Happy Thoughts Playbook

A Collaborative Workbook

Compiled by Kyra Schaefer

Happy Thoughts Playbook

A Collaborative Workbook

As You Wish Publishing, LLC
Kyra@asyouwishpublishing.com
602-592-1141

ISBN-13: 978-1-7324982-0-4
ISBN-10: 1-7324982-0-2

Compiled by Kyra Schaefer
Edited by Rhonda Carroll and Todd Schaefer

Printed in the United States of America.

Dedication

For Vicky.

Acknowledgements

There are a number of people I would like to acknowledge in this book. Shanda Trofe has been instrumental in making this book a reality, without her I don't think I would have had the confidence to keep going forward. I would like to thank our editors Todd Schaefer and Rhonda Carroll they both went above and beyond making this work perfect.

I am so grateful for the magnificent efforts by our collaborative authors and love each of them dearly. You dear authors are the glue that holds this work together and your brilliance shines through in this book and in everything you do.

Including the children in this book was completely inspired. To be so young and yet published brings confidence and self-worth to our kids, and I am personally incredibly grateful for each of them. I know they will create more in their lives. I also wanted to adhere to a quality that Vicky was so fond of – promoting others.

Our young authors are Ciera Bowers (our youngest author at 4 years old), Isaac Bowers and Katie Scala. Your voices and artwork have added joy to this book that couldn't exist without you.

Thank you to the readers who have chosen to purchase and support our endeavor to bring happiness to this world. It is my hope that you will enjoy our journey together and share what you learn here with others.

Contents

Foreword i

Why We Wrote This Book iii

How To Use This Book v

Anytime Happiness Light Passages, Poems, Affirmations 1

We, The Angels By Rhonda Carroll 2
Come Into The Garden: By Bonnie Larson 5
Eternal Joy By Kimber Bowers 6
See The Beauty That Surrounds You By Misty Proffitt-Thompson 7
Ten Habits For Happiness By Misty Proffitt-Thompson 8
You Are Becoming: A Guided Meditation By Laura Rudacille 10
When I Fly So High, Please Follow Me By Bonnie Larson 11
The Mermaids' Chorus By Tonia Browne 12
Be The Light By Misty Proffitt-Thompson 13
What Love Does By Anne Marie Scala 14
The Six Healthy Habits Of Joyful People By Kyra Schaefer 15
Song Of Angels By Rhonda Carroll 17
Hugs And Pizza By Isaac And Ciara Bowers 18
She By Laura Rudacille 19

Going Deep Happiness: Meditations, Emotional Shift, Contemplative Exercises 21

The Plan By Todd Schaefer 22
Divani Tabriz By Rhonda Carroll 24
Curiosity Quest By Lisa Broesch-Weeks 26
Thoughts And Suggestions For Friends And Caretakers By Marion Andrews 30
8 Powerful Steps To Detach From Negative Emotion And Choose A Positive Response
    By Kimber Bowers 34
Return To Joy: The Pieces Of Our Becoming By Laura Rudacille 36
Joy: Dark To Light By Kimber Bowers 40

Happiness Handbook By Misty Proffitt-Thompson 43

Finding Happiness In Chaos By Kyra Schaefer.............................. 50

Accessing Your Joy By Kimber Bowers 52

The Mermaid's Lens By Tonia Browne 54

Tools To Survive The Loss Of A Loved One By Tammy Gamester........ 58

Making Space By Kimber Bowers.............................. 62

Activity Sheets: Coloring Sheets, Activity Fun Sheets, Recipes........65

Food For Thought – To Be Digested In Nibbles By Ronnie Carroll........ 66

Start Each Day With Joy Provided By Giuliana Melo 70

Connect By Ciara Bowers 71

Heart Shaped Word Find By Misty Thompson 72

Jump For Joy By Katie Scala 73

Mosaic: Tree Of Happiness By Isaac Bowers 74

Cooper By Kimber And Ciara Bowers 75

I Am Joy! By Debbie Labinski.............................. 76

I Am Joy Coloring Page Provided By Debbie Labinski......................... 77

Get Happy By Isaac Bowers And Ciara Bowers 78

Hang Out With Happy People By Katie Scala 80

Tower Of Happiness By Isaac Bowers.............................. 81

Rainbow Mug Cupcake By Kimber Bowers 82

Look For Love By Katie Scala 83

Butterfly By Kimber Bowers 84

Self-Centering For Your Happiness By Lisa Broesch-Weeks 85

Recipe for Joy By Kimber Bowers 86

Looking Back By Anne Marie Scala 88

Color, Relax And Enjoy 89

Soul Spot: Deeper Contemplation And Stories About What Happiness Really Is Even In The Face Of Pure Sadness, Fear And Pain 119

Energy Shifting For Happiness By Christine Salter 120

Salvation Declaration By Todd Schaefer 125

The Golden Road Within By Alejandria Kate 127

Are You Little Happy Or Big Happy? By Marchelle Bentley................ 130

All That You Are By Kimber Bowers 134

Finding Beauty By Lisa Broesch-Weeks 136

Joyful Creator By Alejandria Kate 138

My Journey Back To Joy By Tammy Gamester.............................. 144
An Amazing Journey...So Far By Marion Andrews........................ 148
The Fear Of Happiness By Lisa Broesch-Weeks......................... 153

Inspirations: Divine Stories And Intervention, Prayers, Miracles .. 157
Perpetuum By Rhonda Carroll 158
Connecting With Archangel Jophiel By Debbie Labinski.................... 160
Prayer For My Happiness By Misty Proffitt-Thompson 161
Prayer For Acceptance By Kimber Bowers................................. 162
God's Voice Mail By Bonnie Larson....................................... 163
J.O.Y. By Kimber Bowers... 165
Inventory The Pantry Of Your Heart By Laura Rudacille 167
Divine Messages From The Mother By Kimber Bowers 169
Mirror, Mirror On The Wall By Kyra Schaefer............................. 171
Triskelion Provided By Giuliana Melo 175
Joy With The Goddess Aine (Pronounced An-Yah) By Giuliana Melo ... 176

Vicky Memorial And Pictures Page **183**

Author Bios **187**

Foreword

This playbook carries within it the exact energy for whom it is dedicated. Vicky Mitchell was a happy, thoughtful and playful woman. Each time I think of Vicky (and I am serious, each and every time), a joy washes over me and brings a *big* smile to my face. Every...single...time. There has never been an exception.

Well, I guess that's not true.

The day I found out that the spirited student, client, mentee and friend of mine had left her body here on earth and took her spirit to a higher dimension...that day, those first moments, I didn't smile.

Instead, I cried.

I cried for the change that Vicky's son and husband would experience now that she was no longer physically here. I cried for the sadness that our entire community would soon feel as they found out about her transition. I cried for the physical loss of a sister that I was soon to see, but now would not. I cried for the people that were learning from her and would now need to learn from another. I cried for the space Vicky took up in this world so beautifully, knowing that the world would now be void of the Vicky Mitchell that we all knew and loved. But it was at that moment when I thought about the space that her tiny but extremely energetic body took up in this world that I thought about her spirit – her *joy*, her *love* – and I smiled. A *great big* smile came over me and I felt her presence – her "Joy Bunny," energetic, "it's all good" presence. I've been smiling ever since.

There aren't many people who when you think about them they just make you smile, like, *big smile*. That was Vicky. As her mentor, we had many conversations over thousands of topics. She was never short on words, ever. She was the *life* of many of our parties, retreats, writing conferences, events and workshops. Man, did she make me laugh. I think she made a lot of people laugh. She also had the ability to irk a few people, too. I found that amusing as well.

The authors of this playbook have brought to it an energy of their own, integrating love, peace, harmony and joy with everyday life experiences. They give you an opportunity to get out of your head, outside of yourself and into your child within to redirect those thoughts and actions that are no longer serving you.

This book is a compilation of many teachers' beautiful gifts and talents; life lessons and life learnings. I *love* how there are so many different types of teachings and experiences for you, the reader, to have depending on what is needed for that given day: a poem, a coloring sheet, a process, a teaching, a story, an inspiration, a journaling and so much more.

This playbook highlights the exact things that Vicky so highly recommended and believed for herself. We called her the "Joy Bunny" for a reason. As you read and experience the following pages, I believe you will feel the spirit of Vicky. The authors have done a wonderful job expressing their own gifts in honor of Vicky. What I noticed, however, as I read through the pages was that unbeknownst to the authors, they were channeling that life force energy that we knew as Vicky into every single page in this book. Her life purpose and passion are expressed through these light-filled authors who came together, who were inspired to take action, and who created something in memory and in honor of an amazing woman. What a blessed gift to us all.

Enjoy the *play*. We all need more play in our lives. Vicky wouldn't have it any other way.

Sunny Dawn Johnston

World-renowned inspirational speaker, spiritual teacher, and psychic medium, author of 20 books including, *Invoking the Archangels and The Love Never Ends.*

Why We Wrote This Book

Artwork by Dawn Reiffenstein
www.divinesparkart.com

My dear friend, Vicky Mitchell, was killed on March 3rd, 2017 while travelling with her family on a skiing trip. More important than her death was her life. She shined, she laughed, she changed lives and she meant so much to the multitude of communities to which she belonged. She believed in people; she believed in me. When I was lacking confidence or feeling unsure, she required me to pull up my "big girl" pants and soldier on. She always had advice to give (whether we asked or not), but I never felt attacked or threatened by her guidance. I always knew she loved me and wanted everyone she knew to be successful.

As I was slowly waking up on August 7, 2017, I heard Vicky's voice in my head. She simply said, "Write my book." This didn't alarm or trouble me. I had talked to her many times since her passing. This time was different, however – it felt urgent. She wanted everyone she cared for to share their voices with her, one last time. Vicky had several books dedicated to her over the previous months, but that didn't seem like enough.

On August 7, at 7:21 am, I shot out of bed and posted a comment on our "Love and Joy – Vicky Mitchell" online group. This group was created to help us grieve together and remember her in her online communities. (Keep in mind, this group is full of psychics, mediums, health and life coaches, best-selling authors, powerful healers and many more.) I was inspired by Vicky's message for us to write together, but I was met with more questions and concerns than agreement. I had fully expected everyone to be onboard because my motivation to act was strong, but I couldn't communicate my feelings as effectively as Vicky's spirit could.

This led to my self-doubt about sharing Vicky's message. I was shot down often and in a variety of ways, but I knew this project was more important than my fear of failure. But when Shanda Trophe (owner of Transcendent Publishing) said she was willing to help with the project, her support gave me the confidence to keep moving forward. I moved slow and deliberately, and eventually the book evolved into what you see now.

Vicky was fun and funny. She said the "F word" more than I do, and it was hilarious every time she said it. She was a delight, she was flawed and she wasn't afraid to be transparent. She was precious and delightful, and she meant a lot to the authors you will experience in this book.

Vicky's example of being happy, supportive and open about her flaws inspired us to emulate her qualities in this book. Our authors have written about their own happiness, flaws and darkness without apologizing – just like Vicky encouraged.

To experience true worthiness, we can no longer put gold glitter on our unworthiness. Without releasing underlying fear and doubt, we cannot create genuine, lasting happiness. Our authors follow Vicky's transparency and integrity in this book, and we ask you, the reader, to dig deep into yourself and engage the content. As you do, you will reclaim your happiness, your thoughts and your playfulness.

How To Use This Book

You get to choose your own adventure with this book! Let your feelings guide you to whichever section feels best for you to read at any time.

Allow yourself to experience the authors' voices and feel into their respective journeys as they appear throughout the book. You will notice a nice flow as the authors harmonize with one another's messages.

Let yourself feel into the energy of the children's contributions. Follow their innocence and let them return you to your innocence.

Have fun with this playbook. Write in it. Take sections out of it. Hang your coloring pages on the fridge. Most of all, remember you matter, your thoughts matter and you are changing the world for the good right now. Keep going – you can do anything.

Here is a guide to how to use each section of the book:

Anytime Happiness. This is an area where you can easily digest the content and simply enjoy the poems and delight in the illustrations. This section is helpful to read if you are feeling good and want to keep the momentum going.

Going Deep Happiness. This section offers ways to emotionally shift and move your mindset from dark to light with exercises and worksheets. This section is helpful if you feel like you want some workbook time to explore going deeper with yourself in new ways.

Activity Sheets. This is your fun space to color, have fun and simply let your creativity run wild. If you want to stimulate your creativity, start here.

Soul Spot. This important section speaks about hope. If you have been struggling and aren't feeling happy, begin here. It invites you to contemplate deeply as you watch our brave authors learn to choose happiness in the face of pure sadness, fear and pain. True happiness can't arrive unless we personally address our shadow. When we do, only truth remains.

Inspirations. If you are feeling joyful and easy, read this section about divine stories about loving intervention, prayers and miracles. This is your reward for coming through the Soul Spot section with flying colors!

Anytime Happiness: Light Passages, Poems, Affirmations

We, The Angels
By Rhonda Carroll

There are some things seen in darkness
More clearly than in the light
It's your pain of separateness from God
That shows you things aren't right
It's anguish that makes you want to learn
It's heartache that makes you grow
It's uncertainty and bitterness
That makes you doubt all you would know.

We, the angels know your grief
We've felt it all the same
We too once shunned divinity
While lost in the profane
Until we came to see the light
And in it, we saw too
That those who are the love of God
Are all of us and you.

So, embrace the dark; be not afraid
We, the angels gather near
To celebrate all that you are
And your triumph through your fear
Take heart, for in the shadowed depth
If you but reach above
We, the angels are waiting here
To enfold you in God's love.

Dear ones, we've loved you as our own
Since your journey first began
Each time you've cried in despair, "I can't"
We've answered, "Yes you can."
You cannot fail to find God's love
We know this in our hearts
We've cheered and nudged and guided you
Through all your stops and starts.

We, the angels are now the ones
Who feel most deeply blessed.
When you give to yourself your gifts of grace
You give unto the rest.
You are divine; forget this not
When you feel the darkness grow
For we, the angels of living light
Love you more than you'll ever know.

Come Into The Garden
By Bonnie Larson

Come into the garden,
You are invited, pardon.
A meandering path of gold,
The tree of life standing bold,
Weathering the storm, it may,
Shelter others, bend and sway,
Canopy limbs, shade eternal roots,
From the beginning, bearing fruits,
Apple blossom pollen, honey bees,
Hummingbird nectar, 'neath the tree,
Tubular bells, lady's slippers,
Seed bearing plants, li'l dippers.
Butterfly wishes, forget-me-nots,
Fruit filled orchards, apricots.
Dragonfly wisdom, lightness, joy,
It's luminary refraction,
Reflecting light, attraction.
Little white bridge, crosses banks,
Over mystic waters, flanks
Lilies of the valley, baby's breath,
Stargazer heavens, His bequest.
The garden chapel, three bells ring,
For life, the bride, then passing sing,
Paradise garden, heaven 'n earth,
Sweet fragrance, His glory, rebirth.
Lifting spirits, hearts intertwined,
Come into the garden, align.

Eternal Joy
By Kimber Bowers

Sometimes, I am open. Sometimes, the energy of the heavens pours through me and I just let it flow without judgment, without analytics and without discernment of any kind. In these moments, I am aware that I am whole. I am connected. I am supported and I am loved. In these moments, I allow myself to flow in joy.

At other times, I am closed, afraid and hurting. I am a bit lost. I feel this deeper sense of connectedness and yet, for some reason, I doubt it. In these moments, joy seems unimaginable—impossible even.

Through many heartaches, much like yours, I have learned that I am the one who closes. I have learned that love never leaves and that joy never falters, and that only I shut them out. I choose to remain continually open, never ceasing to bloom.

Are you blooming? Can you allow yourself to open? Can you recognize your ability to usher in the light?

Many people use the term joy and happiness interchangeably, but I question their usage. In my experience, happiness has always been fleeting, lasting only moments and generally brought about by something external. A friend tells a joke, a child gives a hug, a taste is surprisingly pleasing, something feels good, a certain song comes on, a certain color flashes or the wind blows oh just so right—happiness is a response. It is a feeling of pleasure that erupts in response to a specific stimulus. We can enjoy it, we can revel in it. It may last longer at times than at other times, but it does pass, as everything external comes to pass.

Joy is much deeper than that! Joy is eternal. It does not fade or falter. It is constantly available. We are the ones who falter and fail to perceive the depth of joy that is available for us to experience and live through.

Joy is a state of openness—a process of unfolding that never ends. Even in the moments when we think we are furthest from it, we are cultivating our own ability to embrace it. Joy knows that there is purpose. Joy knows that there is always support. Joy is never alone. Joy sees only wholeness, releases the past and embraces the present, just as it is.

See The Beauty That Surrounds You

By Misty Proffit-Thompson

See the beauty that surrounds you and invite nature into your life. The flowers become vibrant because of your intense light. As you grow, you become renewed like spring, like a butterfly adjusting to its metamorphosis. Love your true self and others will not only appreciate your beauty, but you will teach them how to appreciate and love themselves as our Creator intended.

Illustrated by Amanda Spratley

Ten Habits For Happiness
By Misty Proffitt-Thompson

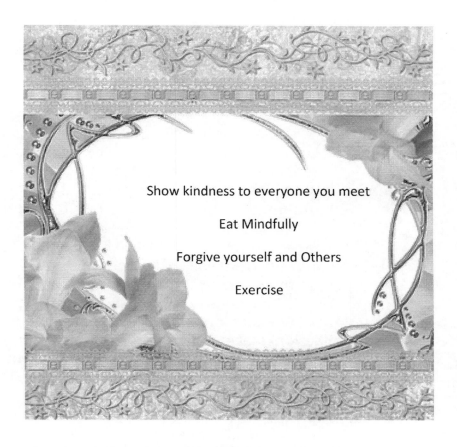

Show kindness to everyone you meet

Eat Mindfully

Forgive yourself and Others

Exercise

What new happy habits will you begin?

You Are Becoming:
A Guided Meditation
By Laura Rudacille

Remember the child you used to be
Expectant of joy and the opportunity to be delighted at any moment
Enchanted by sweetness and simplicity of life
Amazed by bubbles on the breeze, colorful weeds, or shifting clouds
She dreamed in bold color and painted outside the lines
She laughed and explored
Seeds of joy were like wishes from a dandelion
Bring your awareness to the woman you are in this moment
She is everything and is more than enough
She's chased adventure, discovered, and learned
She's fallen down, been hurt, and healed
She looks at opportunity, is cautious, then decides
She is hopeful, giving, and rich with love
She's full of promise and possibility
She takes a deep breath and is delighted once more
She closes her eyes and feels the sun
She lifts her face and feels the wind
Ripe with a revival of wisdom and knowing
Encourage yourself to *be* whatever you need to *be*
In this moment, this hour, this day
You are becoming...

When I Fly So High, Please Follow Me
By Bonnie Larson

When I fly so high, please follow me,
Raising hopes of humanity.
Women and children, gather 'round,
As you hear the voice, surround.
Your sacred voice, Sophia call,
Intention of love, destined for all.
Angels of mercy, so divine,
Taking flight, e'er sublime.
High noon, Noonan, dear heart,
Earhart,
Cameo grace, poised from the start.
Be my guest, you want to be heard,
The quiet voice, confident, assured.
Shooting stars pulsate, resonate,
Sharing their light, commensurate,
Balance your passion, burning fires,
Your light, safe harbor, your desires.
Remember when it rained,
Disappearance n'er explained.
Black is the color, he was detained,
New horizons, transcending planes.
When I fly so high, please follow me,
Raising the coherence of humanity.

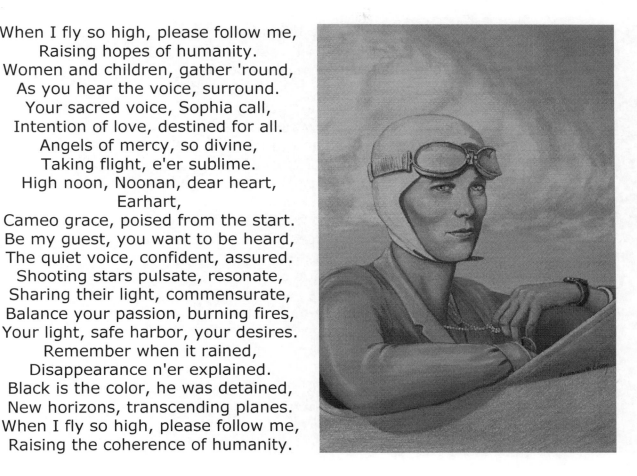

The Mermaids' Chorus
By Tonia Browne

So gently they sang,
in harmony with each other,
their voices hardly audible,
but the vibration increased considerably
so much so
that change was inevitable.
Where as before they had to contain their beauty
scared of captivity,
now there was no other option but to reveal the outward shine of their
glorious hearts,
and to offer the gifts of eternal truth,
They have joined forces with the sisterhood.
So now,
the mermaids sing again.
This time they will succeed
to give the gifts they wanted to share.
They sprinkle their sparkle on the human form
engaging an audience ready to shine,
mesmerizing and stirring a memory,
reminding a new generation of who they really are
and of their power to transform
our age.

Be The Light

By Misty Proffitt-Thompson

Remember how special and magnificent you are. It is inspiring to know that you can ask your angels to reveal signs and symbols that will enlighten your understanding of these earthly duties.

These exquisite beings will be there for you, but you must first ask for their assistance. Be open to receive and believe that you deserve the many blessings that will be shown to you.

Trust and have faith that it is within your sights, happiness comes from within. *Be the light.*

Illustrated by: Amanda Spratley

What Love Does
By Anne Marie Scala

Love heals, not hurts
Love gives, not gets
Love helps, not hinders
Love uplifts, not upsets

Love lights up a room
Love invites to stay
Love lingers in air
Love shows the way

Love trusts and allows
Love flows and frees
Love grows and prospers
Love lives and breathes

Love appears out of nowhere
Love arrives at the door
Love opens up pathways
Love picks up off the floor

Love inspires and encourages
Love takes new flight
Love flies and soars
Love reaches new height

Love gives and receives
Love always shares
Love comforts and calms
Love nurtures and cares

Love moves mountains
Love ignites a flame
Love spreads like wildfire
Love changes the game

Love builds and creates
Love fixes and mends
Something love doesn't do?
Love never ends

The Six Healthy Habits Of Joyful People
By Kyra Schaefer

Have you ever looked around and noticed someone always smiling, always in a good mood and always laughing, and thought, *what is up with them?* Joyful people are not oddities to be examined, but are in a natural state of happiness, the state we can all be in. There are certain behaviors that joyful people perform every day. Those behaviors include living a healthy dietary lifestyle, exercising, and enjoying clean air and sunshine.

Here are six more habits of naturally joyful people:

They Rarely Complain

Complaining does nothing but lets the world know that you are not satisfied with your life and that you would like to perpetuate more of the same discomfort by telling everyone what is wrong and ignoring what is right. There is a difference between complaining and asking for help; one is filling the air with noise while the other is coming up with a plan for the completion of a problem.

They Listen

We can all get caught up in our experience and want to share them with everyone we know, just to have something interesting to talk about. We often lose the ability to simply listen and become aware of the needs of others. When we listen, a new world opens up and we are able to glimpse the realities of others, thereby, becoming flexible and letting go of judgments and limited beliefs.

They Share

Offering a helping hand to those in need, a loving heart and an open mind are all beneficial to someone who may only need a listener. Joyful people offer non-judgmental insights and wisdom based on their personal experiences.

They Put Their Problems Aside

In life, we sometimes experience problems. To some of us, these problems become addictive; one problem creating another. Some people seem to cruise effortlessly down the road of life, while others careen off guard rails. Instead, use a different perspective; let problems come. See them for what they are and allow them to pass by. Get motivated by the solution and stay focused. True masters allow themselves to make mistakes, learn the lessons, and then move on.

They are open to Good Experiences

At some point, our joyful friends choose to be open to positive things in their lives. Their openness creates an outlet for even more positive things to happen, which perpetuates even more joy, until even the smallest experience fills them with laughter and happiness.

They Experience the World Differently

Joyful people experience life in balance, so rainy days rarely trouble them. They may experience temporary letdown, but immediately feel positive again because of some wonderful, yet simple experience.

I often hear my friends and clients say, "I can't find my joy. I don't know what my passion is." My response is simply to remind them to become aware every time they feel happiness. When you examine your life, what part of it brings you the most joy? What part of it brings you the most pain or sadness, and when will the suffering stop? Everything in life is a choice. If you choose to be sad one day and happy another day, remember to choose without judging your choice. However, know that the day can never be brought back. Consciously choosing to bring more good things into your life by modeling a joyful person will help you to begin feeling successful, lifted, joyful and passionate about life. You will feel healthier, clearer, more balanced, and more energetic than ever.

Song Of Angels
By Rhonda Carroll

We gathered together – there were five of us
each with a job to do;
one to love, one to heal,
the rest to follow through
with hope and faith and compassion
to ease the woes of all;
to see to needs before they rose,
to answer mankind's call.
Throughout the ages we have been
God's divine and living light.
For eternity we've guided souls
through their darkest fears and nights.
When we are in service to all those
in anguish and distress
it is our deepest honor
and when we feel most blessed.
For in the core of every soul
there dwells the living light –
the presence of God's spirit,
the flame of eternal life.
This living light we cherish.
We encourage it to shine.
It connects us all to one another,
through the bond of love divine.
So whenever you feel troubled,
in confusion or despair
open your heart to welcome us;
in that instant we are there.
We'll bring to you our touch of peace,
our caress of serenity.
In stillness and in silence
we'll give all we can be.
You may not see our golden light
or feel the flutter of our wings
but if you listen with your soul
you'll hear the angels sing.

Hugs And Pizza
A Fill-In-The-Blanks Story
By Isaac And Ciara Bowers

**Ask a Friend for the different parts of speech blindly, then read the story back to them filled in! Be sure to repeat the word from blank Noun(1) in all blanks marked as Noun(1).

Once upon a time there was a little _____ who liked to give _____ hugs. She would rub
                                         Noun   Noun (1)

her _____against people _____ and chant the words "_____ hugs" while laughing
     Noun(1)   adverb   Noun (1)

_____. Some _____ thought this was _____ but her family
   adverb   noun plural   adjective

appreciated the joy it brought her and thought it was _____, so they gave _____
                                                          adjective   Noun (1)

hugs too. One day, her father ordered a(n) _____ pizza for delivery. When the pizza man
                                              adjective

came to the _____, he was ill prepared for what _____ inside. The pizza had
              noun   verb-past

lots of _____ cheese and _____ on it- the little girl's favorite! When she
           adjective   noun

smelled the pizza she _____ to the door to give the delivery man _____ hugs! The man
                        verb past   Noun (1)

_____ in protest unsure of what was happening! "Don't worry," said the dad,
     verb past

"It's just hugs! She _____ you. We all do!" The entire family started moving
                       verb

_____toward him to give _____hugs, too! He was dumbstruck! But after a few minutes
   Adverb   Noun (1)

the man's bewilderment gave way to _____ laughter! The _____ of the scene
                                      adjective   noun/characteristic

was just too much for him to _____! He started wiggling his _____too! Everyone
                               verb   Noun (1)

was _____these crazy hugs! And from that day on, the delivery men from _____ Pizza
      present progressive   possessive noun

Shop always gave _____hugs whenever they dropped off a pizza. It became their
                   Noun (1)

_____. Only those _____ enough to wiggle their _____a little need order.
   noun   adjective   Noun (1)

Hence, the joy was spread!

She
By Laura Rudacille

She dreams in bold color, she paints outside the lines.
She runs fast and fearlessly, seeing stepping stones
not stumbling blocks.
She's fallen, been hurt, reached for hands, and been uplifted.
She's learning, choosing, deciding;
taking new roads and following through.
She breathes, feels the wind and invites herself to *be* whatever *she* needs to
be in this moment.
She sees the sun streaming through the clouds and embraces each vivid
rainbow painting the sky.
She is delighted and expectant of joy, and with wisdom highlighting her
path...
She strolls on.

From The Heart

What was the most loving gesture you have ever experienced?

Going Deep Happiness: Meditations, Emotional Shift, Contemplative Exercises

The Plan
By Todd Schaefer

There's a way of things, a plan.
A way that few choose to understand.
A noble deed that's been unsought,
Can't be seen by those distraught.

The fire that breathes into your soul.
The mindless chatter of days untold.
A righteous way to see the light.
The choice to be made is always one's right.

What can be said of stories untold?
Can you be brave and courageous? Can you be bold?
Stream your thoughts, silence your mind.
Cheers to the days you decide to be kind.

Why is this, the earth of deceit?
Perspective, you see, is how you compete.
Align yours with His; raise your thoughts high.
Be courageous, be bold, never cast aside.

In your heart you'll know that which you must.
Try very hard, and don't live unjust.
Can you see, what life is about?
No frets if you don't, don't scream and pout.

The mind of the mediocre let's his fears decide.
What he'll do next, in passivity or stride.
The mind of man is hard to grasp.
Transform your best efforts, put them in clasp.

No frets, no fears, no underworld place,
Can reveal the high road, the All-Knowing grace.
Live a life of love, a life of goodwill.
God's word is speaking to you, as you are still.

Wonder about being lost? About the life you can't find?
Calm yourself—silence your mind.
God speaks in peace, and not in confusion.
Accepting negativity is exactly the illusion.

Keep it out of your way, aside. Let it stray.
Optimism is the high road, at least I know this today.
What will the answers be? Tomorrow, or the next?
The thoughts you think now, aren't they complex?

Something's afoot! This just can't be!
My thoughts are my reality! What should they be?
Thoughts that propel you forward, not keep you back,
Are the thoughts you should keep especially intact.

You are where you are. Accept this without question.
Claiming who you want to be, is a start and good suggestion.
So for those seeking to learn, and to understand.
Be courageous, be bold, there surely is a plan.

Divani Tabriz
By Rhonda Carroll

"What does it take to be a master?"
I asked as I drew near;
and I approached him slowly, closer
to ensure that I would hear
his words soft-spoken from his place
perched atop a stool,
I said, "Is there a formula to use
or some unchanging rule?
When does one attain that end?"
And I looked him in the eyes,
"Can a master walk among the living
or must he wait until he dies?"

My teacher sat cross-legged
and he gazed with deep intent
then chose his words, at length with care
to convey just what he meant.
"There are masters living now
And walking on the earth,
old or young, it matters not
in cycles of death and birth.
You seek not to discover
how to do the things we do,
but rather seek to verify
if what you know is true."
He clasped his hands upon his lap
and with the breath he drew,
prepared to tell me what he'd learned
and through the centuries knew.

"When you can taste desire
and not give in to need;
when you can have your every wish
and not be ruled by greed;
when you're awash in deep despair
and yet not drown in grief;
when emotions seize and pummel you

and still you find relief;
when you can face what's just and cruel
with equal strength and grace,
when you're challenged by the impossible
yet you never break your pace;
when pleasures beckon you to stray
from the path you strive to keep
but you won't be caught by ego's lures
or lost to what you seek.
When others destroy in fear and pain
the sacred and the true,
you'll be a master if you give love
with all you say and do."

Curiosity Quest
By Lisa Broesch-Weeks

Oftentimes when I'm working with a client, I notice that as we approach the topic of curiosity and enjoyment, the client may become shy, reserved, and maybe even intimidated by the exercise, possibly because they feel it's too selfish to focus on something that is about them and only them.

So let's think of this curiosity and fun not as selfish, but rather as self "centered"— in the best way possible — because the whole reason for engaging in the activity is to bring joy, fun, challenge, energy, peace, and anything else that makes you feel alive and centered into your life!

Think of your experiences like this: every experience is either a deposit into or a withdrawal from your "bank of resilience." When you add more of what you're passionate about into your daily life, you're making deposits and you're better able to build your resilience. By doing so, you're more easily able to mentally spring into action when you're dealing with the activities and responsibilities that you don't necessarily feel passionate about. It's this Yin and Yang of enjoyment and responsibility that make up the whole idea of creating "balance" in your life. And where there is balance, there is opportunity for bliss.

Use this opportunity to identify your known and yet-to-be discovered opportunities for curiosity and fun. Keep in mind that this exercise is all about you, and is not the place to hold back on what really has the potential for bringing more of what you love into your daily life. I've included sample categories to help inspire your exploration.

Curiosity Quest Exercise

Things you love to do	Things you want to try	Things you *think* you want to try	Places you want to go	Experiences you want to have	Anything else?
Spa!	Taking a cooking class	Sushi?	Italy!	Live in Italy for a month	Take an on-line shorthand class
Dining out	Learn to play piano	Water skiing	Vancouver, BC	Speak at destination spas & resorts	Get to know my son's friends better
Professional	Learn public speaking	Write a book	The new park	Lead a getaway	

Fill in your answers below

Things you love to do	Things you want to try	Things you *think* you want to try	Places you want to go	Experiences you want to have	Anything else?

Were you able to capture a few things you know you'd like to do or try? How about a few things you *think* you might like to try? If so, use this space to set your intention to do at least three of the things you'd most like to do within the next thirty days.

Okay, you're on a roll! Ready to try a little stretch exercise to further your growth? I'm thinking you might be up for the challenge.

If so, continue on...

EXAMPLE:

I will do/try **taking a cooking class** (activity) by **April 30** (date) with **Amy** (anyone joining you?) because I know that doing so will bring more **spice** (joy/happiness/fun/peace, etc.) into my life!

FILL IN YOUR INTENTIONS BELOW:

I will do/try _____ (activity) by_____ (date) with _____ (anyone joining you?) because I know that doing so will bring more _____ (joy/happiness/fun/peace, etc.) into my life!

I will do/try _____ (activity) by _____ (date) with _____ (anyone joining you?) because I know that doing so will bring more _____ (joy/happiness/fun/peace, etc.) into my life!

I will do/try _____ (activity) by_____ (date) with _____ (anyone joining you?) because I know that doing so will bring more _____ (joy/happiness/fun/peace, etc.) into my life!

Curiosity Quest Stretch Exercise

Things you *think* you want to try	With who?	By what date?	Predict your experience satisfaction (0% - 100%)	How much did you actually enjoy the experience?
Try sushi for the first time	My husband	March 30, 2016	I'm 10% likely to enjoy eating sushi.	Wow! I actually kind of liked it; 70% enjoyed sushi.

Fill in your answers below

Things you *think* you want to try	With who?	By what date?	Predict your experience satisfaction (0% - 100%)	How much did you actually enjoy the experience?

Hopefully, you now have a clearer picture of what experiences may bring more happiness and enjoyment into your life. If not, that's okay too – we certainly don't want to give you more things to stress about! You can always come back later to fill in additional pieces of information. You may want to reach out to your family to ask them to remind you of the things that you enjoyed or got excited about as a kid or young adult. You can also ask your close friends to remind you of what they have noticed which has caught your interest. Keep in mind, identifying and incorporating what you might be curious about into your life will now be part of your ongoing routine. Bliss often comes on the heels of passion and engagement, and can definitely bring more happiness into your life!

Thoughts And Suggestions
For Friends And Caretakers
By Marion Andrews

You have just heard the news. Your friend has cancer and will be having treatments for the next six months. You are thinking, "There must be something I can do. Yes, I need to do something to help. But what?"

The first thing to remember is that your friend's situation is about them—not you. That doesn't mean you can't say things like, "I am so sorry that you have to deal with this. It stinks! I hurt with you. I would like to be here to support you." Sometimes, we don't know what to say or not say, so we avoid the person or make an uncomfortable, awkward visit.

Here are suggestions that can help you make the journey lighter for your loved one.

Say the Words: "I Love You!"

Hearing the diagnosis for the first time can be devastating. From my experience, it hit me like a cement truck. Whether you are suspicious of your symptoms or whether it comes as a total shock, you will exclaim, "OMG, how can this be? This can't be happening!" When you are with your loved one, remember telling them they are loved and you will support them no matter what. This is one of the kindest things you can do. Small acts of kindness and thoughtfulness show you love that person, but hearing it verbally is crucial. It is life affirming. I remember thinking, "Even though I have cancer, I am still valued and loved." A hug and a whispered, "I love you" is so valuable. Being there quietly, holding their hand, makes the ill person feel whole.

Make Quick, Frequent Visits and Phone Calls

The ill person may be too exhausted to have long conversations, but a quick hello is always welcome. When I was ill, a question that I didn't like to hear was, "How are you?" But, an open-ended remark such as, "I'm driving by and wondered if I could stop in for a minute to say hi," gives the patient an opportunity to say, "Sorry, I am just lying down for a rest," or "Sure, stop on by." This scenario provides the ill person with the opportunity to be discreet if they are not feeling well. Sometimes, I just needed to say, "I am feeling just yuk!" So, without having to answer the dreaded "How are you," I could choose to verbalize my feelings or not. Don't be afraid to hear these feelings expressed if you are a caregiver—be open to listen and empathize. If you say, "I can't imagine the sick you are feeling, but I am here," it works wonders. I always tried to be as honest as I could when people asked questions about symptoms and side effects, but others may not be ready for that kind of openness.

I have always been a realist and dealt with things head on. If facing something was inevitable, I walked through it knowing it would be better on the other side. I approached cancer, treatments and other indignities the same way. Facing these types of difficulties is a wonderful opportunity for personal growth, but not everyone embraces difficulty as opportunity. Be kind and patient.

Often people say, "Call me if you need me," or "I'm right here if you need something." These general offers are rarely used. It is nearly impossible for a very sick person to call if they need something. It is an overwhelming thought to even ask for something. If you make the offer specific, it is easier for the person to accept. An offer of, "What time can I come and do a quick vacuuming for you?" is easily to welcome. I used to watch the living room rug collect debris because I didn't have the energy to vacuum for even five minutes. I wondered what a great gift it would be if a friend popped-in, vacuumed, or gave the powder room a quick cleaning!

Support Them during Treatment or Tests

Ask your friend if they want your presence during their treatment. When I was ill, I felt it was a huge imposition to have a friend sit with me for four to five hours. Plus, I needed sleep and the space to be there alone so that I could concentrate on visualizing the chemo zapping those bad cancer cells.
Don't be offended if your offer is not accepted. Yet, it is important for the ill person to know that you are present for them—mentally and spiritually—even if you can't be with them, physically. Telling them that you will be thinking of them or holding space for them when treatments are happening is welcome and feels very supportive.

Give Gifts

Bring small things that the person will enjoy immediately. A single flower speaks volumes. A warm and cozy lap quilt or shawl is most welcome. Chemo treatments can feel quite chilly. The ladies of a local church made a prayer shawl for me, which is one of my favorite gifts. They pray with the intention of healing and comfort while they are making the shawls. How cool is that? A funny movie on DVD or even a mixed CD of favorite tunes make wonderful, thoughtful gifts. If you are handy with iTunes or one of the other music channels, making a playlist together is a wonderful gift. Tasks such as choosing music from a long music channel list is daunting. Thought processes are often compromised during treatments. Help is often needed.

Comment on Their Appearance

"You don't look sick or like you have cancer," can be one of the most difficult comments to hear when experiencing a severe illness. What possible response can an ill person give to that? Generally, any comments on appearance are not well received – even "Hello beautiful," or "Hello handsome." Comments of this nature may seem kind but often feel shallow and superficial. Think of other types of compliments like spirited, gentle, resilient, insightful and resourceful. Better yet, comment on what a great friend they have been to you and provide an example of a time when they showed that in a special or even ordinary way. This can be a great morale booster for the ill person. At this time, a patient is usually feeling pretty low and useless, so this type of remembrance is precious. Mentioning other traits you appreciate about them—like having a great sense of humor—is always welcome.

Bring Food

This is a very thoughtful thing to do. Be sure to check ahead of time with the patient as to what they (and their family) can eat. Don't make a tuna casserole because it's easy for you or it's what you have always done. Tuna may be the last thing that she can face or eat at this time. Remember, this is about the patient—*not you*. The recipient feels terrible at having to throw out good food donated with love that they are not able to eat at this time.

What to Do When You Visit

Be aware that you need to be the one to initiate the conversation or suggest an activity. For instance, bring a movie or rent one online to watch together. Sometimes a family member is there to join as well. Watching something for an hour or two is a distraction that will help everyone involved. You are sitting together quietly and yet offering company. Sometimes, it is important to just sit and say nothing. After a hectic week of treatments, doctors' appointments and more, the patient can feel like they've explained their symptoms and feelings over and over, so quiet time with a loving companion is very welcome.

Provide Cards and Notes

I received hundreds of cards when I was ill. Waiting for the mail every day was great! I received many cards right at the beginning of my journey to wellness, but many friends continued to send a 'thinking of you' card at regular intervals. These are especially wonderful. When sending cards, please send a note a few times throughout the duration of the treatments and illness. It means the world to the patient when others are supportive throughout a long journey.

Bringing It Together

It's the little things that make a difference for the patient: hearing those simple yet powerful words, "I love you," getting a card in the mail after three months of treatment, or a phone call from a friend for a quick chat to say, "Hi, I'm thinking of you." These small gestures add up to a giant heap of healing love and kindness to help your loved one get through what likely is one of the most difficult things they've ever had to deal with in their lives. Being there for them—whether it's a physical thing or not—can make a huge difference in their recovery and have tremendous meaning for that patient.

I hope these thoughts from my personal experience over the past four years of this recovering journey will help you in helping another.

8 Powerful Steps To Detach From Negative Emotion And Choose A Positive Response
By Kimber Bowers

When you feel any dis-ease, discomfort, negativity, or stress of any kind in your daily life, follow these steps!

1. **Pause.**

2. **Recall something – anything – that brings you *joy* to break your state.** It can be as simple as a hot shower or a place you like to visit (I like to think about how it feels to hug my children).

3. **Take three diaphragmatic breaths** (breathe through your diaphragm), releasing the situation on the exhale. Trust me, it will pass.

4. **Repeat any affirmation(s) you select:**

> Tension flows from my body
>
> I can relax at will
>
> I am in harmony with life
>
> Peace is within me
>
> Relaxation and peace are always within my grasp
>
> I am filled with peace and calm
>
> I have the power to choose my experience
>
> I can handle this
>
> I am enough
>
> … any other you may choose

5. **Notice your thoughts and feelings** without defining yourself through it.

6. **Repeat 3 and 4** if necessary, allowing it to pass.

7. **Focus your self-talk!** Drop the *whys* and ask *what* you can do in this moment to improve the situation or *what* you can do to use this situation to your advantage. *How* can you grow through it?

8. **Choose a positive perspective** and act from a place of calm and clarity!

Return To Joy: The Pieces Of Our Becoming
By Laura Rudacille

Our expedition through life is like a jigsaw puzzle scattered across the kitchen table in summertime. An individualized journey through a disorganized muddle as one connection at a time we strive to accomplish the idyllic picture on the package.

"Begin with the edges," my mom would say. Our edges: family, faith, love, and kindness; a boundary of security, a foundation to build upon.

As children, contentment and joy were abundant and easy. We were delighted by green grass, blue sky and fluttering butterflies. We lifted our faces to absorb the sun and closed our eyes to feel the wind. We surveyed the myriad of notches and nubs with enthusiastic enchantment. Then with incredible patience we lingered, marrying shape and color—one experience, one choice, and one action at a time.

Opportunity and possibility pulsated in the middle of the table. Color and energy enticed our confident youthful selves to stroll away from the safety of our edges. We raced fearlessly ahead, collecting the pieces needed to fill the gaps. Influence and urgency introduced short cuts, contortion and compromise, bringing life together differently than we'd ever imagined.

Our shape is altered. What fit a moment ago no longer does.

The skewed image leaves us disoriented. Fascination lost, we wonder why we began in the first place. Vulnerable and seeking, we long for simplicity and the return of childhood of joy.

We can't see what we can't see unless we look. We can't know what we don't know until we learn. We are becoming.

"Becoming" is a word my grandmother used. It's a compliment for a young woman to describe beauty, intelligence, and contentment: "She is so becoming."

Seasons of living have taught us life isn't about the precise linking of the visible or obvious. The process of *becoming* is as messy and individualized as we are.

Storms of life have rocked our table. Jarring impacts have damaged our pieces. Vital components have shifted or were ripped away. We've faced the unimaginable and watched as entire chunks of our assembled perfection fell to the floor.

We release the need to tidy and choose, on our own power, to separate from situations and relationships. Unaccompanied but not less, we breathe...restore...and allow peace, patience, and understanding to nurture the fullest expression of who we are *becoming*.

We invite unexpected color, shape, and texture, and embrace flexibility and perseverance. We grip tightly to those we trust for encouragement, support, and guidance. Finding our feet we celebrate the success by simply standing.

Return to the table of your life. Marvel at the intricacy in the picture you've brought together. Take your seat and reinforce your edges. Disengage any portion adding burden and unappealing color. Cut away the frayed, bent, and broken. Observe the open space and welcome the tickle of possibility as the process of your *becoming* ignites once more.

> *"Anything can happen...anything happens all the time."*
> –Penny, from the film, *This is Where I Leave You*

Listen as whispers of subtle wisdom blend with bold certainty, and discover with renewed delight that *all* of your pieces fit perfectly.

Return to joy: Reflect and remember the simplicity of childhood joy. The things within the things: green grass, blue skies, and butterflies in flight.

Return to joy: Laugh from your belly 'til your eyes leak and your sides ache.

The girl you once were has received an upgrade. Her excitement and curiosity has merged with the insight and understanding of the woman you are in this moment—and there is more to come.

Return to joy: Transform, evolve, grow, and step into the adventure of abundant living.

Return to joy: Relax in your truth and release the need to fit the pieces together your way.

Return to joy: Allow tears to flow freely, acknowledging great love and great loss.

Return to joy: Live the highlights of happiness and contentment in all situations. Relinquish worry and concern. Embrace the patience for healing, understanding, and forgiveness.

Return to joy: Step into the wonder and possibility as new pieces arrive and your life's image is revealed, then linger with renewed patience linking one experience, one choice, one action, one connection at a time.

You are *becoming*.

The "Pieces Of Our Becoming" Exercises:

Beautifully broken, forever *becoming*—who you are is everything and it's more than enough.

Reflect over your life's puzzle.

"Look how far you've come;" five beautifully transformative words vital to your *becoming*.

There's a ton of road behind you. You've made mistakes, had wonderful victories, earned a few scars, and built plenty of muscle. Before you seek what's next, *look how far you've come.*

Find your edges and invite goodness, joy and love to fill in your middle. Return to joy and welcome a revival of knowing. Your S.O.U.L. sister of truth (Supportive, Optimistic, Understanding, Loving sister) has waited patiently and is delighted to sit down for a chat. Allow her to introduce you to *you*.

1. Return and redefine your edges. What holds your frame and establishes your foundation? Faith, family, friendship, experience, learning, joy, kindness, laughter and compassion.

2. Seasons of living may have introduced unwanted color and shape. Do you have *open space* to reclaim? Release situations and relationships, worry, or heartache. Trim your bent, broken and frayed edges and enter a space for breathing and dreaming.Compassionately permit yourself to view your feelings in pulsating color. Notice any shades dominating your thoughts. Decide if you are ready to recolor and reclaim the space for a more pleasing shade.

3. Cultivate an *open heart*. Receive pieces of enriching possibility, and vibrant opportunity. Regardless of where you are lying, sitting, or standing, movement is up to you; one experience, one choice, once action at a time.

What activities bring you joy?

What locations would you enjoy discovering?

What new things are you excited to try?

Joy: Dark To Light
By Kimber Bowers

All secrets revealed: Joy is not an end game. It isn't something we attain and our lives become all rosy from that point forward. Life is a little too twisty for that. Joy does not avoid the curves, it simply embraces the thrill of them. Joy is a process of unfolding—a state of opening. Joy acknowledges the beauty of All That Is without comparison to what we may think *should* be. Joy is open reception of the moment.

So how do we get there? How do we tune to that frequency?

Finding joy does not mean that you will never feel sad, isolated, down or frustrated. It means you will no longer get lost in those feelings. You will recognize them as the distractions they are and develop an inner knowing that they will pass. You will tear through the gritty off-road terrain without doubting the existence of the path. You will find peace in the realization that there is reason even in heartaches and earth-shattering moments. You will see your own evolution with certainty.

There was a time when I sat on a dirty wooden floor with a needle in my vein trying to "create reality." I wanted to turn back time, erase the past, and deliver myself to a new beginning, away from the pain to which I had succumbed. I wanted to create my reality, but I didn't know how without abandoning my current reality which seemed to be getting in my way. I tried desperately to escape it. Looking back, I recognize that I had been quite the escape artist. My art, my work habits, my eating disorders, my depression, my suicide attempts, my alcohol and drug use, had all been attempts to escape my current reality when I didn't believe it was possible to create something better.

Finding my joy required me to let go of the need to "create" at all. Creativity is good and "doing" intentionally is beneficial, but happiness isn't about creating something better. It's about *opening to what is here right now*. No matter how scary or painful this moment may be,—*open* to it. Allow that experience to move through you. Just *be* in it, whatever it is.

It is less about becoming and more about un-becoming. It's more about detaching from all the things we *think* we are and allowing ourselves to simply be *as we are*, accepting that that is enough.

Sitting here now on a rock in the desert while my dear friend dies a few miles away, I am sad, but I am okay with that. I am allowing sadness and I am growing through it. This space, this nature and awesome beauty assure me that there is reason and purpose, and that there is grace even in the things my human brain resists.

Can I create an alternate reality where she is not dying? No, I have learned the hard way that I cannot. Can I create a window in my brain that allows her to move on without destroying me? Yes, I can! By consciously deciding to make the space to allow myself to witness the beauty of this moment, to see the frailty of human life in paradox to the insurmountable power of human touch, I can accept what is happening in a way that allows me to navigate this transition gracefully. Acceptance may not make me hurt any less, but it does preserve my joy. Joy is a deep inner knowing that all things are connected and for a higher good. Joy is the inner peace that sustains and allows us to easily move through life's fluctuations. Joy comes from *trust*. Trust your own worthiness. Trust in Source's love. Trust in the love that fuels the greater unfolding of all things that come to pass.

After years of searching for happiness through external roles and relationships, I finally discovered that the key to joy is within me. The key to joy is in my own ability to trust. When I am resistant, when I am fighting, when I am trying to force it to be how I think it *should* be, joy is lacking. When I am open, when I am present, when I take the time to really see the beauty of what is *as it is*, I understand this is exactly what is meant to be. When I trust in that knowing, I have joy.

If you are struggling, ask yourself, "Where am I holding the reigns too tightly? How can I open to other possibilities? From whatever may come of this, how can I grow?" It is okay to want a particular outcome, but not okay to feel that your being depends on it. You are adaptable. Your spirit is infinite. You will survive any outcome (yes, even death). It may not always be easy, but transition is natural and you will always grow through it. Trust in the process. Allow your bloom.

Write A Love Note To Yourself

Happiness Handbook
By Misty Proffitt-Thompson

Part 1: Love

Now that I am older, I have learned and realized a tremendous amount of love. To be loved and to love another means that you can be your true self without judgments—unconditionally. It means being able to show your vulnerabilities in a safe space and know that you are always supported, no matter what. It does not necessarily mean that your point of view is accepted, but that you are respected and heard. It means being able to grow and become a better version of yourself, mentally, physically and spiritually; knowing that your loved ones are by your side cheering you on even though you may be at various places on your journey.

In order to have others support us in the way that we visualize, we must first love ourselves and others in that capacity. It is easy for our egos to tell stories that seem believable about how the members of our family are expected to love us. If I could go back in time, I would be that loving person for my husband, children, grandchildren, and parents; however, all I can do now is learn from this awareness and make conscious decisions daily to follow what I now truly understand.

This is one of my lessons I need to work on because the universe (God) has recently given me several signs. I have received similar indicators in the past, but until I was ready for them, I did not see them. Part of my journey with this subject stems from my morning ritual of reading something inspirational and then journaling about the subject or whatever may come to me. Recently, information I read explained that those around us affect our moods. When I read this, a huge "A-ha!" moment occurred to me. As an empath, I know my mood can affect others and others' moods can affect me. Many others are also empaths (even though they may not realize it), and we must be careful to not accumulate others' negative emotions. I visualize this like baking a cake. The ingredients alone may be plain or primarily used for different purposes. However, when I put them together, my finished product is something beautifully sweet and decadent. Imagine having all that is needed but something unexpected infiltrates your ingredients. It is that negative component affecting your recipe that will inevitably spoil the finished product.

This is how I visualize the impact of negativity from others on an empath like me.

My inspiration arrives when I begin to follow my daily ritual of reading something inspirational and journaling. On the surface, I have known since childhood that I need to treat others the way I want to be treated. But on that day while reading that guidance, I received that message loud and clear. We must remember on this path of life we are all at different points. Some of us have a longer journey, while others have quite a bit to learn in a short distance. Nonetheless, we are here to teach others, to learn from others, and to support each other no matter who they are or where they are on their journey.

While I have this idea of what love means to me, for those in my family, it means something completely different. It's okay for me to continue to have this idea, but this means that is how I must love them. Because our moods can affect those around us and vice versa, it is necessary I remember to ground and shield myself and ask Archangel Michael to surround me with a big blue bubble to maintain my own energy, block all that is negative and allow in only what is positive. This positivity from others will help me witness experiences from their perspective and allow me to grow. When I grow, this raises happiness inside of me. I also ask Archangel Chamuel to surround me with a big pink bubble that reminds me to send unconditional love out while allowing me to receive love unconditionally and graciously, not only from him but from myself and those around me. With their assistance, I can be the light for my family and for those I encounter daily.

Part 2: Joy - Full Moments

Others believe if they find love at such a deep and intimate level, joy will accompany love. I believe joy can appear in all moments under all situations and emotions. It isn't always easy, but it is possible. Be completely present and open, knowing that joy is there. Joy isn't a destination, it is not a place where you will arrive once you have received what you desire. Whether it is a relationship, money or a job—joy is within all things, always.

As I follow my daily ritual, I have noticed that within a two-week span, I have read incredibly uplifting articles that have astonished me to the point of clarity and understanding because of my readiness and openness to experience – and it is now time for me to put those insights into effect. As I allow this awareness to sink in, I am guided to work more deliberately and exhibit my actions from a place of love.

Love is the essence of all things. I believe there are various levels of love, but nonetheless, love is the greatest gift, the most powerful emotion, and the most sought after goal in life we work towards. We all have been heartbroken at least once in our lives. The perceived loss of love hurts, but it also brings an enormous amount of joy, if we only let it in.

As a young girl, I watched fairy tales that showed Prince Charming sweep Snow White off her feet with true love's kiss. This concept solidifies, and as we grow older, we subconsciously expect it from the ones we date. We start looking for fantasy in a partner and it becomes part of our "punch list." This superficial expectation of a partner may sabotage the actual mate (who is looking for you as much as you are looking for them) in finding you. This is what I thought I needed in a relationship so that I would feel full of joy.

Part 3: Love Layers

We have different layers of love, like a cake. When you see a cake put together, it looks so delicious that you get a headache from the sweetness. The first layer is frosting. I visualize our acquaintances and colleagues as the frosting. They are as sweet to us as we are to them, and we must send love their way since they are that spark of light from God. It is only by getting to know them better, by moving through that layer of frosting, that will we begin to see more than just their sweetness.

The next layer is the actual cake. I visualize our mentors and friends representing this layer. At times, they can be rich in love and laughter, bitter if they are having a difficult day, and simple on those ordinary days. We love them because they can be all of this to us and we can be all of that for them. The last is not necessarily the layer, but it is how I visualize my parents, children, grandchildren, and my husband—they are the ingredients. Individually, they aren't the cake; however, it is my family in its raw state that I love, and my family loves me.

Individually we can accomplish wonderful things, but together, we can accomplish amazing things, like creating a cake.

Part 4: My Cuppy- Cakes

We must be present for our children, to show them firsthand the importance of family and the different relationships or layers that we have in our lives. For most children, their parents provide emotional, physical, financial, and mental security while they grow. Children tend to be a little more selfish when loving their parents; they rely on their parents to pick them up when they fall, when they are sick, and when they need any type of support. As they grow older and start families of their own, they begin to realize the mental, physical, and emotional pleasure and pain of being a parent and that they ache to their core for their child(ren).

As our families grow, the love for our parents begins to expand as well. Seeing all there is to do and be makes us look at our parents differently and makes us give them the full respect they deserve. It is a huge responsibility to teach our children right from wrong, to follow their hearts, to be kind, to truly love someone, and to be present throughout their day.

One thing I regret is not being more present for my children. I can learn from that and now I can do more for my grandchildren. We can constantly talk to our children about all they should or shouldn't do. However, it is our actions that will capture their attention. They may not realize it, but they will ever so slightly begin to follow what you taught them.

It doesn't matter how old they are. My older children are beginning to pick up on my newer habits and their actions make me proud. To this day, as the "momma bear," I want to be the one who picks up my children when they fall. It doesn't matter that my oldest is 31 years old; my twins are 26, and my youngest is 15. It is instinct, but I do know that I am not there to fight their battles, tell them what to do or provide for them anymore. My youngest still needs guidance but I need to give her more freedom so she will be ready when she is out on her own.

No matter what, I am here to support them, and I always will. I see what my parents sacrificed for me and my sister, and I truly respect them for what they did for us. They do not give themselves credit and tend to have guilt, shame, and blame for the areas in our lives that didn't turn out suitable based on their hopes for us rather than looking at the things that did turn out right in our lives.

Part 5: Love Lessons

I personally have a wall around my heart and it is difficult for someone to get close to me. When I have tried removing my wall, I've ended up feeling disappointed and extremely hurt. When you trust and believe someone who says the things you want to hear, you believe that their intentions are true.

For me, my intuition told me the complete opposite, but I trusted the person instead, and eventually I got hurt. I allowed those emotions to become a part of me, but I now know that the emotions are not who we truly are. We can begin to heal and realize that we need to let them go (I'm working on this). Placing blame on the person who hurt me suggested I was the victim, and that is not who I am. I cannot put the blame of my past disappointments on any one person—I do believe it takes two people.

At the same time, I allow my emotions to get confused with my true self. I must remember to be the observer, not the absorber, of my emotions. I have realized that people are only being who they are. Most of the time, people are just working on figuring out their lives, just like I am. I do not believe I was deliberately hurt by this person. I know now people are doing the best they can with the information they have at the time.

More importantly, I was the one who put expectations in place by expecting the person to act a certain way. When my expectations weren't met, I felt hurt. I have recently realized this is a form of control. I never thought of myself as controlling, but like everyone else, I did the best I could with the information I had.

Now, I know better, so I must do better. Just because I am now acting more mindfully, will they automatically treat me the way I want to be treated? No, but as I stated earlier, I must treat others the way I want to be treated.

Because we have been programmed the difficult way for so long, we must make a conscious effort every day to develop healthy habits. We must trust, believe, and have faith, that the universe (God) will point us in the direction of our paths and provide us opportunities that will help us achieve what we desire.

Part 6: Happy Tips

♥ Be present. Being present means you are fully aware of your surroundings, and what you are feeling and hearing. Your present moment is engaging all your senses. When talking to someone, looking at your phone, listening to the thoughts in your head or merely daydreaming, could those moments deny you an opportunity to see, feel, hear, or smell something that brings you joy? *You think about the past because you have emotions revolving around guilt and shame. Let the past go.* You cannot change it; you can only learn from it. When you worry about the future you are lacking in faith and trust that you will be safe, but it will work out.

♥ Treat others the way you want to be treated.

♥ Trust your intuition.

♥ Let go of expectations (control).

♥ Be open to self-improvement and growth.

♥ Trust in the universe (God).

♥ Have faith.

♥ Believe that you are worthy and that you have people and the universe (God) to help you.

Journal Questions

Use these questions to prompt your journaling. Do not worry about just answering the questions, dig deep and continue writing...whatever comes up for you write.

1. What does love mean to me?

_____

_____

_____

2. When have I experienced joy?

_____

_____

_____

3. How do I incorporate self-care (love) in my life?

_____

_____

_____

4. What are some of the ways I can show love to myself?

_____

_____

_____

Finding Happiness In Chaos
By Kyra Schaefer

I find it difficult to write a book about happiness. It seems the people of the world are rebelling against each other. There is a feeling of being overwhelmed, and I have to say, it exhausts me to the point of sheer despair.

There doesn't seem to be compassion in the world; there is fear all around. This morning, I learned of the Las Vegas shooting. I wish I could say the first thought in my mind was, "I'm so sorry for those poor people and their families," but it wasn't. The first thought was "Please, make it stop." The shooting was utterly selfish because I am tired of trying to remain positive when there are people in this world who take it upon themselves to kill the innocent who are trying to have fun, hang out at a concert, laugh and be free and relaxed.

I find myself trying to distract and look at my phone to get away from this topic. I just feel like crawling in a hole and waiting for it to all be over, to watch TV and play games on my phone until I die of natural causes like a shut-in that someone finds three weeks after they die. Yeah, that's what's in my mind right now. So, how can I even imagine writing about happiness and joy in chaos? It hurts to even think about making that leap from sadness for our country and our world to joyful, lighthearted reckless abandon.

It's similar to jumping into a pond of icy cold water. At first, the idea seems refreshing, but once your body hits the water all you feel is needles all over your skin and a loss of breath so sharp you wonder if you can make it to the surface without suffocating. It's a push to feel joyful in the face of pain, fear and loss.

I would instead recommend this:

Be with the pain, feel the pain, make it a friend not an enemy. Cry if the tears come; there is no shame in that.

The chaos will likely always be there; it always has been there. We are allowed our point of focus. If it feels good to get involved with the chaos—either through outreach, donation and if you want to contribute to others—do so with a full heart, knowing that you are changing the world.

If you are miserable, powerless or depressed over the conditions you are experiencing, there is hope—there is always hope. It's all we have left, in many cases. It's difficult to get to a feeling of hope when in despair, so start small. What's a little bit better than despair? Maybe helplessness or uncertainty. What's a little better than that? Maybe irritation or anger. What's better than that? Maybe neutrality or observation. As you continue this way, just considering what is possible for you to reach in your feelings, you can glimpse a feeling of hope. Stay in that place for 30 seconds as best as you can. Maybe, just maybe, you will feel the connection to the joy once more. There is no expectation, you will get there in your own time because life and joy always find a way. We are meant to be happy. We are meant to be free.

There is often a feeling of guilt that comes along when others are suffering and we are choosing to be joyful, happy and free. That's normal. We are no longer connected to someone when they are in pain and we are joyful because it's a big emotional jump and we generally want to be around people who are like us ("misery loves company").

We can feel out of place and odd when the world is suffering and we are choosing peace. We will be accused of not caring, not being loving, not being empathetic or not showing up in a way that is joining a fight or a cause—even accused of being lazy or agreeing with the injustice by not saying something. What's potently more dangerous than all of that is losing our light and joy in the face of pain and fear.

We must all do our best to choose love and light in the face of all difficulty. We must be brave and protect our loving nature and argue only for our expansion and not for our limitation. You will find your way. You don't have to jump up and down with elation or force a sense of happiness or try to be upbeat. Instead, feel through the hurt places inside you, connect more often with positive people and let them hold you up to the light of truth; the truth that even in your pain, exhaustion and fear, there is love here for you. It's endless and always present.

Take a breath and let me hold you now in that painful, sad experience, and let us both collectively hold the world and breathe in harmony together. Let's ask that all be made new, and that even in tragedy we can still see, experience and know the joy that is ever present in our hearts. Take another breath and while knowing that you are a light-bringer, continue to shine that light in this world. You are needed now more than ever. Be who you are without apology and love with all your heart.

Accessing Your Joy
By Kimber Bowers

What is joy? Joy is a deep and infinite awareness of your own connection to Source. It is an acceptance of your own worth, an acknowledgment that you deserve love, and an acceptance of all of the ways that love is currently flowing into your life – no matter how separated you may feel from it.

Happiness is fleeting, but joy, once realized, is eternal. Don't misunderstand me, we still have our moments of doubt and that's human and okay, but once we have fully accepted the true state of our own divinity, it is always within our grasp.

How can you return to this state of wholeness, oneness, peace and eternal love when challenged? How can you step into this moment free from doubt, fear and open to trust whatever may come as a possibility to grow your awareness of that endless love?

We all have different ways to help us connect to joy: creativity, music, family, laughter, art and nature, to name a few. These are all good ways to connect, but don't blur the lines. While these things help you get in touch with your joy, they're not joy itself. Your joy comes from within you.

Your joy is in the way you allow yourself to receive love through these external experiences and engagements. Your joy is in your ability to trust yourself and your worthiness, to trust the infinite love of Source, and to trust in the unfolding of this moment without concrete expectation. Your joy is in your ability to be here now and trust that this moment is for your highest good, even when it's painful. Why should you believe that? Because you deserve love and love is always available to you when you are open to receive it!

What does it take to get there? Trust. Think about how many plans have not gone as you expected, and remember what you gained from that process. Acknowledge how different your life would be without the lessons gained through your hardships. Acknowledge that you cannot control any outcome. Stop defining yourself through those outcomes you cannot control. Accept yourself as the spirit moving through you and growing through the lessons offered by them. You are worthy of a new day with new possibilities and endless opportunities to grow. Remind yourself you are still here. You are still living. Accept life for the blessing that it is. Look around you at the beauty of creation and accept that you are part of it. The same energy that flows through the rising sun and the open field is flowing through you.

Who are we to doubt the beauty of what spirit has created? Spirit has created you. Accept that spirit knows what spirit creates! Accept that you are beautiful, too! Open your heart to allow that beautiful energy of spirit to flow through you! You are beautiful! You are worthy! You are always supported! Feel that! Know that! Trust that! Tragedies happen, and so often, we rail against them in an attempt to undo the past out of fear and a perception of lack. We have been created in love. We must trust that the universe brings us experience for our highest good, and open to receive those lessons and live those possibilities. It is then logical to assume that even tragedy serves our highest good. Trust spirit to bring you what you need and support you as you grow through it. When I find myself stumbling into the darkness, I like to ask myself, "Why would a loving spirit bring me this experience? What can I gain through it? How can I grow?" Always there is an answer. Always there is something I can find that allows me to step forward with greater trust.

Joy is in the allowance. Joy is in the trust. Make that choice to surrender the illusion of control. Allow that growth. Allow the love that is always available through opening to the gifts of the experience at hand. Focus on turning any tragedy into a positive ripple through the way you respond to it. Joy becomes yours for the taking—anytime, anywhere.

The Mermaid's Lens
By Tonia Browne

For over twenty years, I have worked with young children and play was an essential part of our time together. Through play, the children learned key skills, concepts and knowledge fundamental to their social, physical, emotional and educational development.

Happy children at play demonstrate creativity and human relationships at their best. They have sparkle, energy, excitement and laughter. As you watch them, you are aware that reality and fantasy merge smoothly. Even actors, improvising a scene, are challenged to match children at play. Give them party clothes and props, and playtime becomes one incredible party. A child can also have similar levels of euphoria when they play alone. The same happy child can be seen communicating with empty spaces, commanding the creation of a responding invisible world, all real to its creator.

There is a positive energy, a contagious excitement and a sense of joy during such interactions. It comes from a place where all is right in the world and anything is possible. We call it "play" and many people undervalue its worth and keep it in the realm of childhood. Is this really where it has to stay?

As adults, how often do you block your own progress or happiness due to your reluctance to imagine a positive outcome? How often do you limit your potential due to fear, or miss an opportunity because you weren't fully present?

My current focus is supporting adults in making shifts in their lives so they can experience more joy in everyday moments. Too often, life can feel out of control and a struggle just to stay afloat. To support changes in perception and shifts in our lives, I use the analogy of diving—diving deep into life. My latest project uses the mermaid to help you explore yourself in depth and to encourage a more playful perspective on life.

The mermaid lens invites you to dive into your life and explore your experiences with depth and honesty. Using the mermaid as a catalyst for change, you can shake off your old stories and let the sparkle of your true self propel you forward with purpose and excitement. It is my hope that through the implementation of key strategies and techniques, you can be in your flow, rather than struggling with the current in order to please others. When you are in your flow, you are in a better position to reclaim your power and to ride your waves with more ease and joy.

Change is coming. We can feel it. Our choice is when to dive and how deep?

A Consideration

- How deep are you willing to dive for a better life experience?

- How big of a splash are you unashamedly and playfully prepared to make in this life?

- What holds you back from making a big splash?

- What encouragement would help you take the plunge?

Benefits of Diving Deep

The mermaid is a label, whether symbolic, literal or archetypical. It is a label to help you understand what can sometimes be contrasting, conflicting and confusing self-help concepts and personal traits. It is by acknowledging and understanding the contradictions in yourself that you are better placed to surf the waves of life, as well as allow the universal tides to surprise you.

Labels are here to help you temporarily. Sometimes the definitions are an extreme and exaggerated version of what you may be experiencing, but by having them presented in such a way, they can assist your development. They can also motivate you into action. Through them, you are able to gain a greater understanding of who you are, where you want to be and also what is preventing your progress.

An Exercise

Find a quiet space where you can contemplate and then complete the following:

- **What tales do you tell yourself that dull your shine?**
  - About your character?
  - About your appearance?
  - About your intellect?
  - About your lovability?
  - About your future?
  - About your past?

- **What do you need to do to put that sparkle back in your life?**
  - Physical changes?
  - Environmental changes?
  - Emotional changes?
  - Other changes?

- **What are you doing that may be impeding your progress?**
  - Over achieving?
  - Over protecting?
  - Over giving?
  - Over working?
  - Over denying?
  - Over worrying?

- **What stories were you told as a child that disempower you now?**

- **What qualities have you hidden, and can these be uncovered again?**

- **What dreams did you have that have been lost along the way?**

- **What did you want from life—your hopes and priorities?**

- **What scares you about life?**

- **What excites you about life?**

- **What did you hope to give back to life?**

- **What makes you laugh now and what used to make you laugh?**

- **What games did you play?**

- **What gives you joy now?**

- **If there were no constraints, how would you spend your time?**

Were there any "A-ha!" moments in the above exercise? Is there anything you had not realized before or had forgotten? Is there something that you could do that would make a difference in your life? Life can often take you in a direction that you may not want to go. Time for deep reflection may seem time consuming in a busy world, but it can save a lot of time and heartache later. We service our cars, have medical checks for our health and spring clean our homes, but we don't always see the importance of doing the same with our minds.

The mermaid's lens represents a willingness to dive deep inside yourself in order to make fundamental changes outside yourself. The mermaid represents the ultimate inner child, as well as the fractious psyche of the personal and global unconscious. This mermaid dances to the tune of eternal mystery, as enduring as love itself. By understanding her needs and wishes, we can integrate the many parts of ourselves more fully and with more compassion.

Through the mermaid's lens we may just allow ourselves to play with life again and find a better flow.

Tools To Survive The Loss Of A Loved One
By Tammy Gamester

Crystals

How do crystals help with healing? Crystals are energy and work with our body's energy field. Crystals vibrate at different frequencies and aid in all kinds of healing. What crystals can you find that are good for loss?

Apache Tears

_____

_____

_____

Energy Work

What is energy healing and how can it help me? Energy work can reduce stress, help you to relax, sleep better, remove blocks and promote healing. Name different types of energy work:

Reiki

_____

_____

_____

Essential Oils

Which essential oils assist in the grief process? Essential oils absorb into the bloodstream and assist in many forms of healing. Citrus oils are very uplifting and can aid in depression.

Lavender essential oil is a calming oil and offers comfort

_____

_____

_____

Grief Coach

A grief coach can be a great source of support and help you navigate the stages of grief. He or she will help you find the insight that is already within you and set action steps for you to take to deal with the loss. A coach can help you find the purpose in the loss and help you on your journey back to joy. What are some ways a coach can assist in healing?

Ask powerful questions

_____

_____

_____

Journaling

Journaling clears your emotions. Putting your thoughts down on paper will help you to move the energy and make space for positive energy. You can write your feelings down on paper and release them to the universe. Some people even go a step further and burn their journaling pages filled with anger, sadness, or hopelessness and send the negative energy out to the universe to transmute into positive energy. What are some journaling prompts you could use?

What am I hanging hope on today?

_____

_____

_____

Mediumship and Oracle Cards

How can I connect and receive messages from my loved one? Seeking out a medium is one way. Ask for recommendations from others as well. You can learn to read oracle cards and receive messages from your loved one. Find whichever decks of oracle cards speak to you and list them.

"Talking to Heaven" oracle cards

_____

_____

_____

Meditation

Can meditation help in your healing process? Yes it can. List a few ways you think it can help you.

Improves self-awareness

_____

_____

_____

Signs

What are "signs" and how do I know they are from my loved one? Signs are anything you see or feel from your loved one. All you have to do is ask for a sign and believe they will send it.

Feathers

_____

_____

_____

Support Groups

Why are support groups so important and how can I find them? Having support in this time of loss is vital. We need someone to help us through our grief. Where do you find support?

Facebook® groups online such as "Loss of a Loved One"

_____

_____

_____

Visitation Dreams

Visitation dreams can come when you are asleep, awake, or during meditation, and they usually happen shortly after your loved one's death. How do you know they are real and not just your imagination?

If they feel real, they are real

_____

_____

_____

Making Space
By Kimber Bowers

My flight is delayed one hour and I've been sitting on this plane without moving. I have to pee! But, we're told we cannot get up! So, here I sit squeezing my bladder and thinking about the one hour of less time I will have to spend with my terminal friend whom I am going to visit – and it's heart-wrenching.

The ice laces across the wing in a sparkly spiral pattern of water and light, and I allow it to move me. I allow myself to be assured that my time is not always right. I think about the network of spiral patterns – of touch and expansion – that propel our lives. I close my eyes, and I sit back, trusting that the day will unfold exactly as it needs to.

My heart expands with an overwhelming sense of gratitude for my friend's touch on my life. While four days of reconnecting may not seem like quite enough to honor a lifetime of support, I know that the impact she has had on my life is infinite. She is in me. She is with me always. Her touch on this world expands infinitely through all whom she has touched.

Through this infinite space and trust in its larger unfolding, I find my joy. I recognize my own wholeness and open myself to whatever may come.

Joy fills the space. It is in the opening, the allowing, the growing, and the touch. When we are able to release our expectations (whatever time schedule or order of events that may have been) and accept what is here for us to experience in the moment, we open ourselves to new possibilities for growth and new realizations of deeper awareness we may have otherwise overlooked. Had I wasted my energy thinking about my need to pee and feeling angry about lost moments with my friend, I would not have experienced the deeper appreciation inspired by my current surroundings and my willingness to be moved by what is here for me right now and I would not have this reflection to share with you now.

Mountains with peaks, valleys and slippery slopes exist within you, always rising again. Trust that transformation. Trust that while mountains grow, and break, and crumble, they remain rock. You too, are solid. You too, are growing. And you too, will break. But, you will grow and take new shape and rise again! Step back from the negative thoughts, limiting expectations, and dependent attachment that interfere with your happiness. Make a space through which deeper awareness and connection can come. Open to the unfolding even when it looks nothing like what you may have expected or hoped for. Allow the possibilities. Trust in the transformation. Joy is yours for the taking. Keep walking through the valley one step at a time, trusting in the rise. It will come.

Happy Notes!

Activity Sheets: Coloring Sheets, Activity Fun Sheets, Recipes

Food For Thought – To Be Digested In Nibbles
By Ronnie Carroll

- When there is no resistance, there can be no force.

- One must overcome the complex to conclude the simple.

- When you deny responsibility, you limit freedom.

- Confusion is nothing more than an indication that your belief system is about to change.

- We live by intent. When our actions reflect our intent, we feel balanced and at peace.

- Forgiveness is feeling with love what you once felt with pain.

- We identify ourselves by our relationship to all else that exists.

- Spiritual connectivity is not limited by distance. It's determined by resonance.

- Both the controlled and the controller are equally tied together.

- Avoidance doesn't keep you isolated from unpleasantries. It only keeps you in denial.

- The amount of fear we feel is in direct proportion to the amount of love we block.

- By placing judgment on your own state of being, you create a point of reference from which you judge all other things.

- All true power is self-generated.

- The objects of our angers are never the causes of them.

- Expectations open doors for disappointment, invite control, and dictate our reactions to events before we experience them.

- Guilt is the only weapon of control for which the victim determines the severity of force.

- Your own persistence is your only true indicator of your belief in yourself to succeed.

- The most difficult thing to argue is not undisputed authority, but unbridled ignorance.

- Failure isn't a finish. It's a line to be crossed.

- Mastery is the ability to make continued improvement.

- It's not difficult to be remarkable if you believe in yourself.

- There is more harm done through anger than through human error.

- If you want the freedom of choice, you must also accept the responsibility of making choices.

- The key to wisdom isn't in answering the questions, but in questioning the answers.

- Those who feel powerless, resort to force.

- Nothing exists without your consent.

- To find spiritual centeredness, one must overcome a belief system of duality.

- The greatest act of tyranny is using the promise of freedom as a weapon of control.

- We seek to control those things we feel powerless to change. We seek to change those things we feel powerless to control.

- When ego insists that we label ourselves, it is demanding that we limit ourselves.

- The future exists only in our imagination. The past exists only in our memory. When you worry about the future or regret the past, you cannot live in the present moment. Since there is no other moment to live in, how would you define your existence?

- Knowledge is answering the questions. Wisdom is questioning the answers. Enlightenment is experiencing the wisdom.

- Many people believe they feel at peace because they don't have any problems, when just the opposite is true.

- Love does not have to be reciprocated to be love. If reciprocation is a requirement, or love is traded for a favor or an object, then love has been made into nothing more than a tool of trade with no more value than what it is being traded for.

- You will never find unlimited peace, love, or joy looking for them from a perspective of limitation.

- The greatest masters have all felt fear and self-doubt. It was by overcoming these that they attained mastership.

- If you feel a need to justify your action(s), ask yourself if you are acting in accordance with your true intent.

- If God gave mankind "free will," why can't we give it to each other?

- The most common weapon against fear is anger. Angry people are frightened people.

- If ego is the false self, what other than a false reality does it have to offer?

- Anything that can be measured can be limited.

- Until we give up our desire for strife, we will continue to experience it.

- Any time we justify any negative emotion, we remove all desire to overcome it.

- Gratitude is its own state of grace.

- Every sense of loss is fear induced.

- We cannot learn to accept until we learn to detach, for how can we reach for the new while clinging to the old?

- Laws in and of themselves are powerless. It is only the fear of punishment that gives them power. So, why would an all-powerful God need the threat of hell?

- The two most important lessons I've learned: #1 Learning to trust the voice of my soul and #2 Learning to listen to it.

- If you want more out of life, put more in your heart.

- Can anything we do be a sacrifice if from it we receive – in any manner or to any degree – a reward?

- Inspiration is a by-product of contemplation.

- How tragic when we confuse elation with joy, indifference with peace, and validation with love.

- Judgment is the precursor to condemnation. Condemnation is the antidote to self-loathing.

- Free will doesn't mean choices with consequences. It means choices.

- When it comes time to make a tough decision, some people will find all sorts of ways to complicate the issue.

- Walking on eggshells to avoid upsetting someone isn't love or friendship. It's co-dependency.

- There are two kinds of people in the world...you're not none of them.

- We owe a debt of gratitude to the insane, for they have endeavored to show us that *all* reality, no matter how delusional, is merely a construct of the brain.

- All forms of control require enslavement.

- Fetal-position mentality is a direct result of knee-jerk thinking.

- If nothing anybody else does is about you, wouldn't it stand to reason that nothing you do is about anyone else?

Start Each Day With Joy Provided By Giuliana Melo

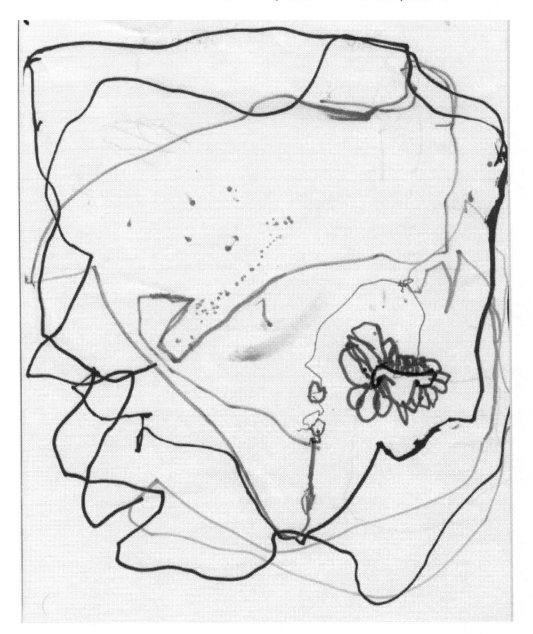

Connect
By Ciara Bowers

Our young author/artist Ciara (4 years old) drew this just for you with instructions. "Use your pencil to continue drawing and connecting lines. Then color between the lines, and cover with dots!"

Heart Shaped Word Find
By Misty Thompson

```
        N D Z V Z L                          M L O V E P
      W T T K B U L J K                    R Z E T S D K M A
    L N U K I X W D Q A E                O D V L G R R N L L O
    Z C E F D E V B R Y T N E          B P O H M L A J G G O I Z
  A S V G B F J E L H Z O V V C      Z V N A J C I Y A U M X U A Z
  R K P F M M K G K X K E B C W      D K P W K Q H I U C E T J M B
  Z Z S X E K L W F H T I A F F S D  B H P Z S W Z I A Q V B V I M V S
  N P I W B N K T K L L G V D C V T K   I G I G S E L F C A R E C Z Q X W L
  O S B U F G Q X V E R J V S S U X Q Y Q N X D J Z R B X Z A N U P G P O U
  P F W Q L B F B B K B X A I K F J U O E N F A Q Q C X V D D C X N I W T A
  T G U W D I X A Z Y Z W G N N R J E S T S N P A N N S I C F E W V Y Z V E
  H K R B R Q Y E L F Y W U Y F T E S Q Z F P O C Q R P L J U R U T S J K P
  K B D L S A W D A T B T G H O N U D E P D R R A E D I Q B T H R W Y D Q X
  K Z W V F O V N Z P P V I K O J T I O C V S F V E K R A U G W O G Y O X E
  D D V D B D Y X H E D K V L O N X L T C R W C X A U I F S K A C P U W R K
  R S W G M U O N I I A Y M I P N L T I Y S P I O K T F Z R Y O B E K W
  G P X L F G C T K S G E D C B V F P A O J O U P E U X L X I M O Q E F
  B W T P J J P J F C H X C I G A T V K O N K N V K A O B W H K A K T C
  X P W G A C H J Y O P T W Y Z R S K H L W Z H S L V J A I I Q C E
  M H E U X V U H C W U T I F O N E N Z V P O N E V L Z K Q O O D M
  M S L L R T W P Z X J O L A C U N F D B M A K X Z M R D V Z Y
  S G C H W S K B G X T C O U D S Y L N P B T S W N Z P A B U F
  Q U K I U W H X A Y Z R F F A X B U P C X L K H V N A A N
  H W K H R D D U U D I S N K D Y B L V M O P N O X G M O C
  S Q W T S G S J V A T J A L N L K Y W X E D B V W C C
  N S B E K F J M E D C S Q G I W X G C M L W M N H
  R O J M Z I O O E V M J R V U M E A G P I X N R K
  Y I H M M A S I G T G Q T E P R A E S U K X S
  D T J S H U Q Q Y N R E Y X B N K R W Z C
  K A M Z J O W K Y K A T H I M Y W H Q
  L T N E S E R P Z M V A C B H V X
  V C P X V B A Z Z M S G F V D
  C E N G R O W T H Y E E W
  M P G A Z A E O A F O
  U X H Q D L Q P T
  S E T M W P T
  N O R F N
  F U D
  N
```

WORD LIST:

BELIEVE	HAPPINESS	LOVE	SPIRITUAL
EXPECTATIONS	HOPE	MINDFUL	TRUST
FAITH	INTUITION	PRESENT	VULNERABILITY
GROWTH	JOY	SELFCARE	

Jump For Joy
By Katie Scala

Mosaic: Tree Of Happiness
By Isaac Bowers

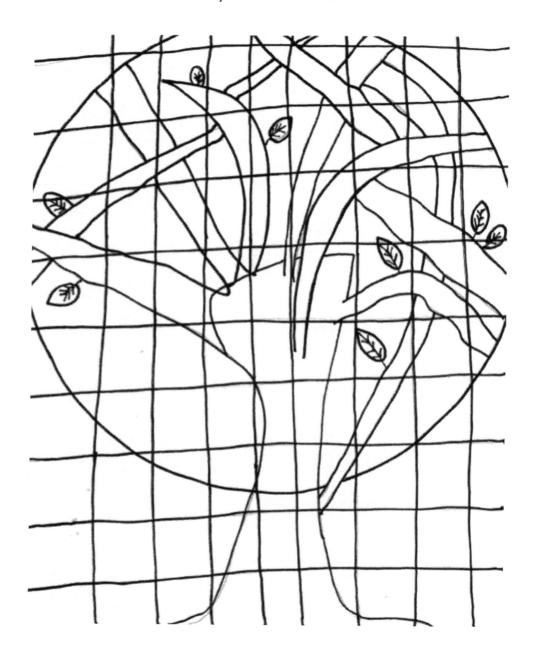

"Happiness is a mosaic of diverse experiences fused together in a full and beautiful expression of our own light."

~Kimber Bowers

Cooper
By Kimber And Ciara Bowers

"Can we just cut off his hair and put it in the book?
That fluffiness would make people happy."

~Ciara, age 4. Model: Cooper

I Am Joy!
By Debbie Labinski

Joy is a fairy who lives among her nature friends. She is here waiting for your invitation to grant you a transforming wish. She offers a nurturing calmness for you. When you look at her beautiful blue eyes, you can instantly feel trust.

She likes to sing you a song of joyful delight to raise your vibration. "You are joyful," she says. Joy is here to ask you, "Do you believe joy is a gift that has been given to you from spirit?" Joy and her magical friends are here to offer you guidance.

Whatever animals you are drawn to immediately give you a personal message. The firefly tells you that the magic of life is yours. You are enlightened. Can you see your inner light? The dragonfly will guide you to see your own magic and light so that you are able to empower others to be open and happy within. The butterfly is a beautiful reminder that you are in a time of letting go of your old self or experiences of whom you thought you were meant to be by this time in your life. The frog is here to remind you that you are ready to jump to the next place in life; that wherever you land, it will be magical. The frog is firmly holding onto the mushroom but he is still looking forward like he's ready to let go. Are you ready? The frog wants you to know it's time to live a vibrant, sweet and magical life.

Are you in a state of emotion or contemplation of the next leap to take in life? You are in the process of transforming. The biggest message here is to let go of the past and let your intuition open now and enjoy the process. Now close your eyes and visualize where you are taking that leap of faith. Where are you going? What are you doing? What do you see? How do you feel? These are the questions you need to ask yourself while you are taking that leap of faith.

All is well. The message that joy is here to give is to live your life in the most wondrous and magical ways. She wants you to know you are ready to let go of the past, that it is time to transform your dreams into your new reality and to always remember to say, "I am joy! My life is a gift!" And so it is.

I Am Joy Coloring Page Provided By Debbie Labinski

Get Happy
By Isaac Bowers, Age 9, And Ciara Bowers, Age 4

My sister and I have made these lists of things that help us get happy so that you might get some ideas from it when you are feeling sad. Feeling sad is horrible and I don't like it, but by thinking of things that make me happy I can find happiness again and calm down. Maybe making a list like this of your own could help you, too!

Isaac's List
Happiness is....

The soft touch of a fluffy animal
The crackle of buttery popcorn
The suspense of a good book unfolding
Time spent with family
Witty puns
Creating with friends
Making things happen through the art of coding
Swimming in soft, cool water that makes me feel stronger
Uncontrollable laughter
Wading in the river and discovering all it holds
Swinging (feeling like I can fly)
The stillness of sitting on a strong rock
The air beneath my feet as I jump from rock to rock
The excitement of fast rides
The awesomeness of mythical creatures (dragons, phoenixes and the like)
Imagination (feeling like I have the ability to make things out of nothing)
Feeling loved
Pizza and popsicles
Swimming in the ocean and playing in the sand
Thinking about things that grow
Red and blue
White snow
Being in nature
Exploring new things

Ciara's List
Happiness is...

Hopping like a bunny
Loving & hugging
Fluffy puppies
A cold drink on a hot day
Playing with friends
Making things for people you love
Orange drinks
Listening to whistles
Pretending! (Because I get to do anything!)
Dancing!
Meeting new friends
Slithery snakes and snapping alligators
Climbing trees
Riding a horse
Playing in the sand
Finding sand crabs
Pretty flowers
Pink everything
Jumping in the water
Playing with a dog in the snow
Ice cream and strawberries!

Hang Out With Happy People
By Katie Scala

Tower Of Happiness
By Isaac Bowers

I have drawn some things I am grateful for that make me happy on top of this building: my family, colors, and a goofy, furry monkey! You can draw some things in the windows that make you happy! Any time you are sad, you will have this picture to look at and remind you of all the good, happy things you have to be grateful for in your life! Have fun!

Rainbow Mug Cupcake
By Kimber Bowers

Here's the thing, I really don't like encouraging people to find happiness through food, because it has gotten a lot of us into trouble! However, there are occasions when I want a treat or simply want to play a little, and the kitchen is always a great place to play and create! I love cooking because I learned how to be passionate through watching my grandmother move to her own rhythm in the kitchen. Because I'd watched her, I don't generally use recipes (including this one). I simply tend to feel my way, throwing in a shake of this and a shake of that, and learning from whatever result I get. For the record, this is a cupcake recipe that no one has to feel guilty about. Yes, it contains fat—but healthy fat—with extremely low carbohydrate content and no sugar or artificial sweeteners, which means you will get an indulgent treat without that spike and crash traditional sugar gives you. Your body will thank you for it! This recipe is also extremely versatile. You're not going to screw it up. You can add any flavors you like to it: berries, cocoa, lavender (or any herb or spice), lemon, fruit juice, any kind of extract. The options are many! Plus, you get to be whimsical with the colors, all in a matter of minutes. Have Fun!

Rainbow Mug Cupcake

1 egg
2 Tbsp of melted coconut oil or butter from grass fed cows
1 Tbsp unsweetened nut milk, coffee or other liquid depending on your mood
2-4 tsp of coconut sugar depending on preference
4 Tbsp +2 tsp of ground flax meal (replace 1T + 2tsp with cocoa powder if you want chocolate)
1 tsp coconut flour
1/2 tsp vanilla or other extract
1/2 tsp baking powder
Pinch of salt
Food coloring

Melt the fat in the mug and mix in the rest. Add in any nuts, seeds or chopped chocolate you desire. Drop in colors you desire a few drops at a time and swirl them around with a butter knife or skewer. Microwave for one minute. If still moist, microwave an additional 15-20 seconds at a time until done. Voila!

Look For Love
By Katie Scala

Butterfly
By Kimber Bowers

Self-Centering For Your Happiness
By Lisa Broesch-Weeks

Self-Centering for Your Happiness.

It's how we think about and process our inner feelings that creates or negates the ongoing struggle.

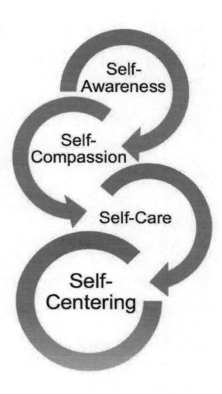

- **Self-Awareness**: Acknowledge your feelings, remember that being imperfect is being human. It's ok to feel hurt, frustrated, angry, lost, etc. Feel it and then move forward. Forget telling yourself you "should" feel or think (or be) something else in the moment.

- **Self-Compassion**: Self-criticism **undermines** motivation (not the other way around). Our response is often to shut down/feel depressed—which isn't useful. Instead, practice being **present in the moment rather than being perfect** in the moment. People who have more self-compassion are linked to feeling more happiness because they don't waste energy on anxiety & criticism. Treat yourself as you would treat a friend in need of compassion. Ask yourself *"What can I do to help?"*

- **Self-Care**: When someone (including YOU) treats you poorly you feel bad and begin to function poorly. **Instead,** rest, create "down-time," implement boundaries, listen to your instincts, seek out hugs, watch & listen to positive stories and videos. View every stressful and worrisome or painful experience as an opportunity to practice being mindful. When you create new thoughts, you create new beliefs—and ultimately, new realities.

This quote from Dr. Kristin Neff sums it up beautifully. *"When self-esteem desserts you, self-compassion should step in. Self-compassion allows for the benefits of self-esteem without the pitfalls of self-criticism."*

Exercise: Planting the Seeds to Flourish

In what areas do you feel your "inner critic" may be excessive? On the lines below, write down some examples of where and how self-criticizing may be harming you. Example: *I find myself constantly comparing myself (personally and professionally) to others and it's robbing me of my happiness.*

_____

_____

_____

What habits or thoughts can you eliminate (or begin) to improve your self-compassion and care, starting now? Example: *I resolve to build myself and others up, rather than knocking myself down, by looking for what I love and appreciate about myself and others and eliminating the tendency to hone in on "imperfections."*

_____

_____

_____

Recipe For Joy

By Kimber Bowers

Ingredients: detachment, self-acceptance, alignment, openness

Materials needed: oven, giant pan, processor, values

1. Preheat oven to any temperature you please. (We're not really cooking anything here.)

2. Line a pan (a *big* one) with a lot of *joy.*

3. Prepare the detachment by placing all of the things you think you are, into the food processor fitted with an "S" blade. All of the roles, responsibilities, physical qualities or abilities, jobs, relationships or anything else you may define yourself as, gets thrown in. Turn the processor on "high" and process to a fine sand that can be easily sifted. Recognize that this does not hurt you but is more to allow malleability (you will "fit" in more places, anywhere); you are still standing. Think about how much more you are than any of these things.

4. Pour in some self-acceptance. Look at who and where you are and what you may have been validating yourself through. Recognize that you do not need validation. Accept yourself as a work in progress. Accept the beauty of your own becoming. While you may be all of these things, none of them defines you. Pulse a few times to incorporate the self-acceptance into the surrendered identification, creating a paste-like dough.

5. Ask yourself, "What is really important to *me*?" Get in touch with your own values. Decide to honor them in all you do. Find your alignment and lay it in the pan.

6. Press your dough into the lined pan any which way you choose. Do it in a way that feels good to you: all to the side, all in the middle, evenly spread, haphazardly thrown—your call!

7. Acknowledge that you have no idea what you just created or how it will work. Accept it as okay because you will learn from this process! Open yourself to all of the possibilities of what *is* as opposed to the expectations of what you may have thought was supposed to be.

8. Put it in the oven until it's done (cooking time may vary; months, years, lifetimes—there's no guarantee).

9. Taste! Enjoy the experience and what you have learned from it! Get a little closer to a full and clear expression of all that you are!

Looking Back
By Anne Marie Scala

Turning fifty years old means different things to different people. For me, it was an invitation to reflect on where I've been and who I want to be, moving forward.

What I've come up with can best be described by a song that's almost as old as I am. At times in my life when troubled waters threatened to take me out, a bridge of hope and encouragement always appeared and lifted me up. Now, when seas get stormy, I know to look for a bridge.

And when it's smooth sailing, I will do what so many have done for me. I will be a bridge.

Reflection questions

1. Many times, a bridge of hope and encouragement appears in the form of a friend. Can you recall a time when you felt completely overwhelmed and a friend showed up as your lifeline?

2. Bridges can also take the form of words. Can you remember a time when you felt lost and a quote, scripture or sentence flashed in front of you and offered divinely timed direction? Where did these words appear? On a billboard, bumper sticker or your computer screen?

3. Whether it's the classic Simon and Garfunkel version or the Josh Groban & Brian McKnight duet, the song "Bridge over Troubled Waters" is a compelling example of how music ministers to me during moments of distress. What are three songs that lift you up when you are feeling unsettled?

4. What does the intention of "being a bridge" mean to you?

Color, Relax and Enjoy

Soul Spot: Deeper Contemplation And Stories About What Happiness Really Is Even In The Face Of Pure Sadness, Fear And Pain.

Energy Shifting For Happiness
By Christine Salter

As a spiritual practitioner, I have spent a large portion of my life trying to figure out how to make being a human easier. In my journey, I have discovered that we all have different paths set before us when we are born that help us to evolve and grow as souls. Many of us face challenges and obstacles to work through that seem to stretch us to our limits. We might be well versed in pain, sorrow, struggle or fear. We might believe that the only way to get somewhere in life is through hard work and struggle. We unconsciously choose to learn through pain because that is what we believe is our only choice. Most of our time is spent in survival mode just trying to get through the day, and it leaves little time for fun, happiness, or even joy.

One of the gifts of being human is free will. We are born into a paradigm set forth by our families, but as we evolve and grow, we are free to add new beliefs and release ones we have outgrown. The challenge with growing and changing is that the ones we love may not be on the same journey. Everyone is on a unique path and people may come and go in your life. The universe or spirit uses this as a lesson to teach you about trust and acceptance.

One of the main lessons on the road to happiness is in regards to resistance. I have found that when we are in resistance, we're not at peace and certainly not in a happy space. Resistance means that we're not trusting the process of life, and we're trying to be in control of things well beyond our control. The truth is, the only thing we can control is how we respond to things, but we like to feel like we're doing something. Something is better than nothing, right? Or, is it?

Resisting means that you are energetically fighting what you don't want. It steals your peace and leaves no room for happiness. The more we push away the circumstances in our lives that we are unhappy with, the more we experience those circumstances. We might constantly think about our lack of finances or the love that we are missing, for example. The more we sit in the energy of what we perceive to be lacking, the more of that energy we experience, thanks to the *law of attraction*. The law of attraction states that whatever we put our attention on, we will receive more of it. The phrase "What you resist persists" perfectly sums this up. The first time spirit gave me the message about not being in resistance, I stepped into resistance even more. I was afraid that if I stopped resisting, things would never change for the better. Spirit showed me how wrong I was.

When spirit brought me the idea of acceptance, I stepped right back into resistance. I was not happy and it terrified me to give up what control I thought I had. Spirit taught me that acceptance is the opposite of resistance. They said that acceptance doesn't mean you are agreeing to—and will be stuck with—whatever you don't like in your life. It simply means that you acknowledge exactly how things are, without judgment. Acceptance breaks the cycle of energy that keeps us stuck. We stop fighting what is, and allow what will be to unfold. It requires learning to trust spirit to bring you what is in your best and highest good. It allows peace and happiness to start to bloom in your life. Acceptance allows you to go with the flow of your life instead of swimming against the currents. You will end up where your soul intends and you can get there by the pain of resistance or the joy of acceptance. This is your choice alone to make.

Making the shift from resistance to acceptance requires raising our awareness of our inner, unconscious world. Our inner belief system dictates what we experience in our outer world. If we believe that life is difficult, then we experience difficulties. If we think people are mean, we experience mean people. We are unable to draw to ourselves and our experiences the things we think we really want. We have placed ourselves in an invisible box and sealed it up. We are frustrated that life isn't working and we don't realize that we have the power to free ourselves.

The first step to freedom is acknowledging how you have chained yourself. Your first instinct might be to think you have played no part in your circumstances or you are victim to them. That is the perception of your ego or lower self. All of your life experiences have put you squarely where you are today and you are exactly where your soul wants you. It takes a lot of courage to look at how you participated in your current circumstances. This is where your power is. You can get to peace and happiness by shining a light on the places in your life that you feel aren't working. Once you accept where you are, the energy can be shifted. Just remember, there are no judgements to be made here. Judgement is giving your power away. Everything is divinely orchestrated and this exercise is meant to empower you to make the changes necessary to improve how your life feels. All that is required is that you are open and honest with yourself.

The next step is to explore where the emotional energy is stuck in your body so that it can be released. Frustration, fear, sadness, depression or anger are just a few emotions people might experience when their lives aren't working how they want. When these unprocessed emotions remain in the body tissues, they can eventually create pain and illness. It is important to acknowledge these feelings and notice how they show up in your body. This will require tuning into your body and noticing how you feel and how your body feels.

Emotions can be stored in any part of the body. People typically store them in their abdomen, chest, shoulders, back or jaw. Everyone is unique and yours might show up somewhere else. The way emotions feel to people can differ. Emotions can feel like tension, tightness, pain, heat, heaviness or discomfort, as examples. Yours might be different, and that is okay. Clearing your body of heavy emotions will create a new path to experience peace and happiness on a regular basis.

The last step is actually working with the energy to change it into what you desire. As an energy healer, I have spent years helping people tap into the energy of their emotions. The emotions will have certain characteristics that can easily be shifted. You will be using your imagination to "look" at the energy. I will ask you questions and the first thing that comes to mind will be correct. There is no need to second guess it. Once an aspect of the energy has changed, the shift takes place and the healing begins.

It is important to do the following exercises with an open mind. You will be working with unconscious energy and it won't always make sense to your conscious mind. I will walk you through steps that require you to use your imagination. The most difficult part might be not judging what comes into your mind. You will acknowledge it from a detached perspective, but you are not to dwell on what comes up. Dwelling on it will keep the energy "as is" and the goal will be to shift it. As things come up, you are to let them go, trust the process and your soul who guides you. You will choose one area to focus on and you can repeat this process with other areas as needed until you feel complete. Focus on one issue at a time, starting with the most pressing. Before you start, take out a sheet of paper and answer the following questions. Allow yourself to go into great detail in your answers, writing down whatever comes into your mind.

Step 1

Is there a part of your life that you know you need to change or are frustrated with? Take a deep breath and let an insight pop into your mind. Write down the answers to the following questions:

Describe one area of your life that is not working for you or you find very frustrating.

Name the reasons that you think it isn't working.
List what you have done to change it.
List why you think it hasn't changed.
What happens if this isn't resolved?
What is the main emotion you are feeling right now?

Step 2

Think about your problem and feel the main emotion in your body.
Using your imagination, feel where it is showing up.
Where in your body is it showing up? Is it in your head? Jaw? Heart? Abdomen? Other?

What does it feel like? Tightness? Tension? Heaviness? Pain? Other?

Using your imagination:

What color is the energy of the emotion?
What shape is it?
What is its temperature?
What is its size?

Still using your imagination while connected to the energy:

Change the color of the energy to another color.
Change the size of the energy.
Change the shape to something else.
Adjust the temperature if you want.
Make any other adjustments that feel good.
Allow yourself to come back gently to full consciousness.

Bringing in Peace and Joy:

Another energy practice that I personally use regularly quickly shifts your energy to the frequency or emotion that you want. This exercise uses your imagination and can be used daily. You can choose any emotion for this exercise, such as love, serenity, peace or joy.

Take a few deep breaths and allow yourself to relax.
Take another breath and think of the word "peace."
What color comes to mind? The first thought is the correct one.
Now think of the word "joy."
What color comes to mind? The first thought is correct.
Imagine the color for peace is shining down on the top of your head.
Breathe that color into your body, filling up all of your cells.
Imagine that color flows into the energy around you, filling it up too.
Now imagine the color of joy flows into you through the top of your head.
Imagine it filling up your body and the energy around you.
Imagine you are full of both colors and they swirl within you. Feel the energy of peace and joy in your body.

When you are ready, open your eyes and gently stretch.

The work that you have just completed is simple, yet powerful. Changing the energy in one aspect of your life quickly makes shifts in other parts. It is wise to work only on one area at a time because as you shift one area, the others will automatically begin to shift. I recommend that you work on one major area at a time such as a relationship, career, or finances so you don't overwhelm yourself with too much change at once.

Shifting your feelings about challenging aspects of your life can be easier than you think. Once you decide to accept where you are, you are empowered to make a new choice. Your chains are gone and the changes you make will be permanent. The way that you used to struggle will dissolve and you will step into a flow of ease that you have never experienced before. Peace, happiness and joy will become more abundant and you will draw to yourself the experiences that you really want. Spiritual growth and healing are a journey and don't happen overnight. Be gentle with yourself as you grow and trust that everything is happening for your highest good. Your soul loves you very much.

Salvation Declaration
By Todd Schaefer

...And so we begin to gently choose light. And we feel a sense of power from that light. We feel a small shift. We feel that we are no longer feeling as bad as we once were feeling, so we decide to choose again into that direction. We decide to continue marveling at that power we just displayed where we were previously making a choice that was in absolute darkness, and we realized that even in our misery and pain, we finally found something—our power to choose.

Our emotions begin following this choice, and we reinforce more and more to ourselves as we rise up that we are seeing ourselves in our greatest glory, that we are using our most profound definition of strength, that we are remembering ourselves while in our darkest hour, and that remembering ourselves in our darkest moment, and our power to choose, is the greatest display of divine power that we could hope to know of ourselves.

This is our divinity, and it is more powerful than anything else we know about ourselves. And if we remember, from when we were in the complete darkness, we were still present with our true selves, in all of our glory and power. And we knew, deep down underneath us, that the real us was there somewhere, and that we just had to be our true self while we were in that space long enough to know the real power that we are.

...And so our minds begin to change dramatically at this point. We begin to realize how helpful our pain has been to us, and how much our struggle has meant to us. And we remember this choice that we made while we were feeling at our worst. And, we remember that while we were feeling our worst, we had the ultimate opportunity to empower ourselves to be our best.

The best that we can be for ourselves is choosing to remember who we are when we have forgotten. When we feel no incentive and our world tells us that there is no way we can make that change, and everything in our feelings tells us the same—we still choose.

Only when we feel the absolute darkness within, can we truly experience how bright our light truly is, and that no matter how dark it gets, our light never, ever burns out.

(Excerpt from "Our Salvation Declaration," from *The Acceptance Guidebook* by Todd Schaefer)

The Golden Road Within
By Alejandria Kate

In life, we often get caught up in our own pain. Constantly on alert and in survival mode, we're like soldiers on lookout for danger. Sometimes in protecting ourselves, we focus so intently on keeping the wall up that we don't recognize the love trying to penetrate our barriers. In addition, we miss opportunities to be of service to one another.

I have found that love is the trustworthy road on which we can venture out into the world. Everyone has their own story, their own fears, and an inner torment that hounds them every day. If we can separate from attachments and find freedom in the great peace within, we will discover that inner serenity is the greatest love we can know.

I've started looking at others and seeing them through their pain. When I do this, a love sprouts forth within me and compassion swirls within my being. In life, we tend to take things personally when, in reality, another's actions has everything to do with their private journey. We can serve another better by trying to understand them, by being slow in our knee-jerk responses, yet quick in our extension of love and kindness.

Nature has so much to offer us in wisdom. A seed blooms with darkness, water, sunlight, and nurturing. The seed must first be dropped into the darkness for future bloom. From the help of the elements, and ultimately, the power of self, the seed breaks through its hard shell and blends with the soil around it before rising to the light.

Part of the human journey into a spiritual awakening is spent walking in the darkness. But is it really darkness or lightness being unearthed within us? Healing can be a painful process, but new growth prevails. Many of us have been hurt and wounded. A journey inward on the golden road brings forth a lightness of being, a love for mankind, and a glory and appreciation for one's self that outshines the chaos.

The golden road within isn't easy and requires a commitment that only the journeyman can live up to. There will be challenges that bring one to their knees and tears that bathe the soul. But the sunrise and sunset of each day give life to our heart's ever-expansion.

Letting go of attachments is a golden key of awareness. We don't own anyone—a mistaken belief that some people make. Families are gifts. Spouses are gifts. Our friends and every person in every situation, no matter how painful, are gifts.

Some gifts float into our lives like beautiful dandelions, softly touching our lives. Other experiences roar and shake us up a little bit. All experiences serve us. Trusting and surrendering into the gift sends out waves of gratitude. Everything moves us along.

We own our choices, our mistakes, and our misgivings. Other people are simply other journeymen finding their way on the golden road within. The sooner we let the attachments go, the brighter the road becomes.

As travelers on the golden road, perhaps we should focus on the light within and outside us, embrace how expansive that light is, and know that there is enough for everyone. Let go of our attachments and desires to consume. By clinging, we can inadvertently bring more pain into another's life, keeping a cycle of dormancy that serves no one.

Trust in the light and make space for others to walk their golden road separately, each of us in our own light. But we are *one*, and on a singular journey to the same place.

If we don't own people but only own our choices, what are we?

Perhaps we're the sunlight on a dewy morning leaf, or the cry in a newborn's wail, or the buzzing of the hummingbird's wings. Maybe we're everything that breathes and everything that cries, and in that knowledge lies the power we all have: the power of love, and the knowing that we're all one. In that knowing, love bubbles up to help us rise.

Be the light and walk in the light. Love with all your heart. And when life knocks you down, bow your head, plant more seeds, and rise in love.

Are You Little Happy Or Big Happy?
By Marchelle Bentley

Don't tell your children anything – ask questions. Don't tell your children to be the best. Tell them to be the best just for today. Our children will already face enough challenges in life, so adding extra pressure will do nothing for their confidence. One thing that my child went through when she was young was the death of a classmate and friend.

When Ashley* was 6 years old, all the children in her class were scheduled to go on a field trip. Ashley was very excited, as were all the children. She went to school as she normally did, happy and interested in learning something new. She did not know the heartbreak that awaited her arrival.

The teacher announced she was preparing for the field trip but had some sad news. All the children listened intently. El Jermain, a classmate, had perished in a house fire along with his brother. This news saddened all of the children, but Ashley was inconsolable. No matter how badly she wanted to stop crying, she simply couldn't. Her teacher tried to make her stop crying by saying, "We are all going to have fun today, and you will be fine." But Ashley shook her head, and continued to cry.

As Ashley was travelling home on the bus, her teacher called me about El Jermain. The teacher told me that Ashley had been "disruptive" all day on the field trip.

"Are you calling me so that I might punish her?" I asked.

"You need to have a talk with her," she said in an interfering tone.

"Are you trying to tell me how to raise my child?" I said, but before I let her answer, I hung up without a word.

Ashley's uncle Hank worked at the fire department close to where El Jermain had lived, and where the subsequent fire had taken his life. I called uncle Hank to ask him if he knew anything about what happened. Interestingly enough, uncle Hank had been on that call and he carried out a small boy who had died that night. I told him that the boy was Ashley's classmate, El Jermain, whom she had lunch with every day and loved very much.

As a parent, you have to pull from the deepest parts of your soul to help you explain to children that bad things happen, even to other children. Finding ways to do that can be the most challenging and heart-wrenching pursuit.

Although Ashley knew about the concept of death (because her father died when she was 3), it didn't make it any easier to help her understand death when it comes to a child and a close friend. This is how she and I came to terms with this tragedy.

I always read to Ashley, and when I did I tried to help her see other things, not just the lessons in the book. To help her understand death, I told her that everyone has a book of life. Some books may be long with many pages, some are medium sized and some only have one page. Every book is important, even if it's short. Helping her to have seen that life is impermanent (before this tragedy) was valuable. She knew nothing was wrong with death; it was a part of life and it is okay to cry, especially if the book was very short.

When Ashley got off the bus, she and I sat down on the front steps. I looked at my daughter still catching her breath from sadness, her eyes still full of tears, and I said, "You and me, we've got this one, Ashley." That is when I told her that I had called her uncle Hank, the firefighter.

"I talked to your teacher and she told me about El Jermain," I said to my little girl, who was so full of sadness. "When did you feel the saddest today?" I asked her.

"He missed his snack time, and his lunch time, and one snack on the bus ride home," she said with big tears falling on her cheeks.

"I'm going to tell you something, and when I'm done, I want you to tell me if you feel 'little happy' or 'big happy.'"

"Okay Momma," she said.

"Do you know uncle Hank went to that fire and put that fire out? Oh, yes he did!" I said and she smiled. "You know what else he did?" I said.

"What?" she replied.

"He carried El Jermain out of that fire."

"He did?" Ashley's eyes widened.

"Oh, yes he did!" I said.

There was a pause and Ashley smiled.

"Why are you smiling?" I asked, uncertain. Then she said something I will never forget.

"Momma, I'm smiling because uncle Hank took El Jermain to heaven."

I had to pause for a moment at the profound innocence of this child. She loved her uncle Hank. She loved El Jermain. In her mind, knowing that her uncle Hank was there meant even though El Jermain was dead, he wasn't alone.

"Now Ashley, answer me something. After learning uncle Hank was there for El Jermain, are you little happy or big happy?"

A smile grew across my child's face. "Big happy," she said.

"That's very brave of you. Do you want to go to McDonalds?"

Ashley nodded.

"Get in the car, let's go," I said.

The next day when she got off the bus, I asked her, "Did you feel little happy or big happy today?"

She responded, "Big happy. I didn't cry at all, but I was sad at lunch time."

My daughter grew up and is now 40 years old. She still remembers El Jermain. To this day, she appreciates that I ask her questions instead of telling her how to think or how to feel. Neither a child nor an adult can feel good when you tell them they will be "fine." Everyone has their own process. They have to explore in order to understand who they are, and they determine when they will be ready to be "fine."

All anyone can do is be their best today. Ashley did her best with the loss. I did my best to help her navigate it, and together we were able to find our "Big Happy."

*Marchelle Bentley is Kyra Schaefer's Mom. Kyra is Ashley's pen name. This article was originally written as a Eulogy for Kyra's Cousin Travis Grodski who passed just before this book was completed.

All That You Are
By Kimber Bowers

There were years of my life when I didn't even believe that joy existed. From a place where every waking moment was a struggle that I felt I simply could not endure (addiction, suicidal, clinical depression), I have come to a place where I am now teaching others to have a more positive outlook on life. Looking back and remembering how harrowing every moment of my existence was at that point in my life seems so completely far away from me now. Yet, I remember the feeling and I know it was real. *Your* feelings are also real.

What changed? How did I get from there to here – a place where I am joyful? How have I created a space for myself to be happy and content and at peace regardless of anything that's happening around me, regardless of the losses and the heartaches (which still come)?

It was a process of unraveling. I had put all of my purpose, all of my validation for being into caring for the man that I loved, and when he passed away, I watched all of my dreams and all of my hopes disintegrate with him. My entire purpose had been swept away, but I somehow was still standing, which led me to question my existence. In that questioning I began to unravel all of the things through which I had identified myself, and I recognized that I was none of them. I recognized that my existence did not depend on any of my roles or accomplishments or relationships. Knowing the power of this great universe, there must have been a reason for me to exist just as I *am*. How are you defining yourself that limits the realization of *all you are*?

With all of those external layers expunged, I began to go inward and recognize the spirit that I really am, the spirit that is growing through all of it. When you begin to recognize that there is a part of you that is none of the things you think you are, your entire perspective will change. You will want to live in alignment with that deeper part of yourself. That spirit—when you align with it—will lift you into the light.

As I made outward changes to reflect my inner being, I became more aware of my own thought processes and sought to change them. To be honest, I wasn't very nice to myself. One by one, I stripped away the self-judgments that had led to my misery. And then I began to strip away other judgments as well. Releasing the need to classify anything as "good" or "bad," and simply allowing myself to *be* with whatever is.

134

I opened enough to see my own spirit in all its worthiness and I accepted the beauty of everything just as it is. I found hope and I found *trust*. It was a slow process of training my brain to process things in life differently; to see and accept every experience as a possibility for growth, to see and accept every moment as a gift of love from source. But, I had *no* idea what I was doing! I was grappling my way out of a dark tunnel with no light. *Today, there is light!* Today, there is a whole book of light! Use whatever you find in this book that resonates with you! Get in touch with that inner spirit and seek to align yourself with it. This is where joy is found!

Finding Beauty
By Lisa Broesch-Weeks

Some time ago, I decided it was time to tame my tropical (and very overgrown) backyard. I had a vision of unearthing the potential I knew it had, and I was on a mission. In this intense labor of love, I spent more than 75 hours hand-pulling weeds and ferns, trimming palm trees, cleaning my wooden fence and re-staining my pool deck. I had almost conquered the jungle and felt incredibly satisfied, but there was one thing left to do: cut down the massive 14-foot hibiscus tree that was taking over a good part of my (and my neighbor's) yard. You see, I had always hated hibiscus. I know—how can anybody hate hibiscus? I can't explain, though—I just did—a lot. So I set off to chop it down and kill it.

So I'm out there, lopping off branches and sawing off parts of the trunk (I even had to get a chainsaw involved), and as I chopped away at the branches, I tossed each one into a pile. When I eventually cut off the final limb, I turned to look at the enormous pile and said to myself, "Hey, those flowers are really pretty." Suddenly, out of nowhere, my sense of accomplishment turned to guilt and remorse. I felt terrible about cutting the tree down to nothing. How could I have purposely stripped away something so beautiful without even realizing what I was doing?

I quickly snipped the flowers off the branches and gathered them into a vase. When I stepped back to admire them, I was so moved that I actually started to tear up with emotion. The flowers were so beautiful; and to think, I almost threw them out with the trash.

I suddenly wondered how many times I had done that to myself over the years. How many times have we all done this to ourselves? How many times have I chopped away at the gifts and beauty I've been given, never really understanding why, just continuously (figuratively) hacking away at the parts of myself that I felt weren't good enough? I never truly appreciated the extensions of my personality, strengths and talents that have been right in front of me the whole time.

Sound familiar?

That day, I vowed to myself that I would consciously choose to find the inner and outer beauty in myself and others rather than waste time cutting myself down. I won't lie—the temptation is usually there, and I still hear from my "inner critic" on occasion. When I do, I remind myself of something one of my coaches told me: "Integrity means that you're in the right relationship with yourself." I have always loved that quote, as it grounds me and reminds me to listen to my inner wisdom. If I "hear" something that is useful in building myself up, I take heed. Otherwise, I shut it down. I encourage you to do the same. Don't wait until it's too late to turn back and appreciate what you've had all along. You can start right now to notice and appreciate all that is beautiful in you. Beauty comes in so many forms, both inside and out. Recognizing where your beauty lies, is the first step toward creating and culminating self-compassion and ultimately, bliss.

Remember, not only is it okay to love and take care of yourself; it's essential to your overall well-being. So let's see where you may have some room to expand your self-care and self-compassion.

Joyful Creator
By Alejandria Kate

There are times when we find ourselves in conflict with our thoughts and emotions. Situations don't always work out the way we hoped and another's actions leave us emotionally traumatized and/or stuck in a negative state of mind. From our perspective, we've been wronged, and when in this mindset, it's hard to consider another alternative.

Some of us may be fortunate enough to receive an apology, and we're able to build our confidence, let go of any grudges we may hold, and move forward. But painful situations where no apology is extended leave us picking up the pieces with our emotions in turmoil. How we choose to perceive a situation determines how our thoughts align. Positive thinking makes a difference in our attitude and gives birth to inner peace, joy, and happiness.

When we're willing to step outside of our emotions and open our perspective to a new direction in thinking, possibilities for joy become endless, and a previously unknown frontier in our mind appears waiting to be explored. We loosen our grip on "being right," and open ourselves to acknowledging the formation of the endless creativity. Realizing we have control in how we think opens a doorway to a new way of experiencing life, experiencing people, evolving ourselves and living in a state of joy.

We come to understand that it is how we perceive our circumstances that impacts our joy, and we then can take responsibility for how we greet each challenge. This becomes a game changer in our reactions and interactions with others. Breaking down the barriers between ourselves in love is the first step to building a new foundation.

Each of us has a belief system that determines what we perceive to be right or wrong. We're reared in a way that builds a thought process and through this structure we navigate life. Usually our belief systems are taught to us as children either by our parents or our experiences. The trouble with belief systems is they can be chains holding us in a prison of emotional pain.

Imagine a belief system as a pair of eyeglasses. How one sees the world is visualized through our spectacles. Everyone wears eyeglasses and none are exactly alike. These eyeglasses have been handed down through the generations. Some eyeglasses have become outdated. The lenses are cloudy, and peering over the edge of the eyeglass lenses to see the world through one's own eyes is similar to the action necessary to create a new belief system.

Questioning one's reality is the way to think outside the box. Are we our bodies? Are we our identities? Do our jobs and wealth define our value? Or are we more than our bodies, more than the cars we drive, and more than our physical attributes and life experiences?

If we're more than our bodies, then what are we? And if we're more than our bodies, then do the things we currently value lose their worth in the perspective of the larger picture, including the grievances we carry?

Seeing beyond the physical opens up a highway to the divine intertwined in countless beautiful moments.

When we turn that divine eye inward, we see beyond our physical bodies and into the emotional dimension of our inner being. Hidden beneath our earthly cloak lies the light of the soul. This light is the universal power that binds us and the love of spirit that connects every living being.

We can will the light to come forward, and within that sacred spiritual space, the physical falls away. Some find this peace through meditation. Joy bubbles up as attachments fall away. In the space beyond the physical, one can feel like a leaf on a tree swaying in the wind; yet, simultaneously feel like sunlight filtering through the tree's branches.

With detachment to the physical and mental sphere comes true happiness. The emotional turmoil of the physical life falls away and a blending with the spiritual realm happens. Peace rises and love and joy come to dwell within the physical vessel where the soul resides.

If we're not our minds and our bodies, then how can the grievances of life have true meaning? Are these disputes and disagreements based in reality at all? By the truth of the light within, we find that blame has no meaning other than to teach us, and through sacred detachment, the light will prevail.

This sacred space can be elusive and requires practice to maintain, but it's a road within that is based on the fundamentals of our choosing. We can decide the way we perceive life and how we understand every experience determines the level of our joy.

Finding joy in detachment may seem like a counterintuitive route, but stepping away from an old pattern of thinking and pursuing the opportunity of personal growth in every situation can be akin to removing constrictive shoes and wriggling one's toes in warm sand.

Emotional pain can feel like rocks carried around in our boots. Weighing us down, their burden is heavy, and for some, moving forward becomes impossible. Thus when trapped in our own pain, self-pity steps forward and our joy can become squashed between anger, resentment and a big dollop of fear.

Living a joyful life is a choice; it's surrendering to the universal power within us. Seeing life in a black-and-white manner makes experiencing rainbows impossible. Just like settling under a fluffy blanket on a soft couch while watching the rain outside a window, observing sorrow as separate from us, like the raindrops on the windowpane, can be wonderful.

Love is a white fire within us all and by its illumination we can warm our souls. Beyond the illusion of the physical body dwells our soul, and beyond the soul is a universal spiritual power that connects us. That power is a creative strength each of us can tap into at any time. Embracing ourselves as the designer in our lives is a new way of thinking that can open doors we previously couldn't perceive.

Like a flower closing to the moon and blooming to the sun, we thrive in light. When acting as creators, we can blend into the white light within and send that light without. It is a choice to bloom or to wither.

Letting go of painful offenses can feel impossible, but if we dig into that pain and plant new seeds of thought, a forest of possibility awaits us. Offenses can feel personal and it's common to internalize another's projection. If we look deeper, we find that what we project out is reflected back, and what we consider a grievance can become a map to personal healing. It's our responsibility to gaze into the light of our own soul, find healing, and view the world through the perspective of love we are all composed of. Learning to tap into our creative power and dwell in the space of love is the key to living a joyful life.

How do we create joy? By choosing our thoughts in a way that builds a bridge to inner happiness. Like soiled clothes we remove from our bodies, it is our responsibility to remove negative thoughts from our mind. Holding onto anything that does not positively serve us is equivalent to taking a bath in a mud puddle.

It is the individual's responsibility to siphon nutrients from the dirt of negative experiences. They are our gifts of grief. But simply removing a person from our lives doesn't always eliminate the negative emotions, and some situations make it impossible to remove an offender. Chaos may arise. Carrying negative memories in our mind is equivalent to sipping a flask filled with poison.

If possible, remove negative individuals from your circle of friends and family. We may have to break up with someone who causes disruption to our harmony. We may have to shut the door on family members. Physically removing negativity is a positive action. Afterward, mentally place them in a beautiful land created in one's imagination and close the door.

Dealing with other people in our lives may require more complicated decisions. Perhaps we share a child or we have a negative coworker or a bullying classmate and cannot extricate ourselves from the situation in the near future. It doesn't serve us to focus on a negative situation we cannot change. When forced into an unhappy environment, it is better to keep our thoughts positive until we can change our circumstances

In either situation above, maintaining a positive focal point is essential. Divine light exists in every soul. Discovering the light within another in a way that allows our own soul to bloom yields many benefits, including a positive mindset. Seek the good in an individual and hold that viewpoint steady in your mind and heart.

We are all born creators. The people in our lives are actors in our personal play. For individuals who have caused us grief, it may be easy to simply find an amiable memory to replace the sorrow that lingers. With another, finding an immediate resolution may seem impossible. Instead, invent one. Use your imagination and make a positive memory. Use that memory as the blueprint for any person who has committed what you may consider an offense against you.

The last step is mental training. We must train our minds to focus on the positive memory we have attached to this person. That should be the only event we allow into our minds.

The people we have removed from our environment can no longer inflict pain unless we give them that power. It is through the use of our mind that we hurt ourselves, so we should master our thoughts in order to practice the attributes of a strong character. When unhappy ideas float up into our consciousness, turn your thoughts instead to the positive concepts you have put in place there.

For those people and experiences that remain in our physical surroundings, expect there to be challenges, but train the mind instead to focus on a positive attribute of the offender, and when in their company, detach from the present to instead enter into that positive world of your creation. The mind can become a haven of beauty.

This technique isn't an act of denial—the offense against you happened; it hurt, and it is what it is. For some it's still occurring. Some environments are beyond our ability to change, but we can change our reaction to them. The fact remains that there are people in our lives that have caused and currently cause us pain. But the bigger reality is that we're spiritual beings having a human experience, which makes this world illusory, so the answer is to rise above our grievances and invite in joy.

Holding onto a painful memory or stewing in emotional torment doesn't serve us. Removing the cause of our pain, whether physical or emotional, finding the lesson it brings, integrating it into our lives, letting that experience help us grow and then releasing the negativity while moving forward in a positive mindset keeps us in a process of joyous expansion

We are not only our bodies; we are instead beings of light that are composed of love. Reaching for the light within another via a perfect blend of detachment and love makes for a rising of joy and light. Be in the world but not of it and trust in the folding and unfolding of your own light.

Write A Letter

From Your Future Self A Year From Now. What Successes Have You Had Over The Last Year.

My Journey Back To Joy
By Tammy Gamester

"I guess Heaven was needing a hero
Somebody just like you
Brave enough to stand up for what you believe and follow it through
When I try to make it make sense in my mind
The only conclusion I come to
Is that Heaven was needing a hero like you"
~Jo Dee Messina

The most tragic event a parent could ever imagine happened to me September 1, 2014. It was the eve of Labor Day and I was up late reading, knowing I didn't have to get up early for work the following day. I'd spent a quiet, uneventful and relaxing weekend with my husband, John. At 11:00 p.m., the cell phone rang; my son, Tim was calling. He and his brother Josh had been in a car accident. Emergency personnel were working on getting Josh out of the car and taking him to the hospital. I quickly awakened my husband, explained the situation, and started packing for the long drive from Arizona to Texas. I was anxious but not overly worried. Everything was going to be okay.

We'd packed the car and were ready to go when the phone rang again. This time the caller was Josh's dad. He said that Josh didn't live. He'd died at the scene of the accident. *No*, it couldn't be true! He couldn't be gone. It had to be a mistake. I fell into a state of shock and disbelief. I had been prepared to sit in a hospital room with him while he recovered—not going to see him for the last time. As I write this, my gut hurts and tears roll down my cheeks. Even after three years I still feel the wrenching pain in my heart beyond imagining. Josh was only 24 years old. He had his whole life ahead of him and in a split second it was all gone. He was gone.

The drive to Texas that night was made through tears and disbelief. So removed from my Christian beliefs, I couldn't even pray. I was numb. I remember getting as far as Tucson, an hour and half into the drive, and I said to my husband that there was no hurry to get to Texas now. I couldn't believe my baby was gone. I would never talk to him again, never hug him again, never see him fall in love, get married, have children. The finality of it all hit when I saw him for the last time. He looked like he was asleep. I just wanted to shake him and say "Open your eyes and look at me. This is just a bad dream and you are okay." But he wasn't okay and it wasn't a dream. It was my new reality without my child in my world.

Josh was an online gamer and he was learning to write computer code. He loved racing and cars and was creating a racing game. I regret not asking him more questions about what he loved to do. In my mind, he was too withdrawn—a loner who needed to spend more time with people. What I didn't realize was how connected he was to others online. There was such an outpouring of love from people whose lives he had touched. One young man from India reached out to me and shared how Josh had impacted his life. The online gaming community, where he played, created memorials in the games for him. The community's response was incredible and humbling.

Family and friends held a memorial for him in California. My expectation was that I would be sobbing, but I experienced just the opposite. Everyone shared wonderful stories about Josh, and we laughed together – truly celebrating his life. His four best friends from high school and two from junior high school were there and they shared stories I had not heard before. After everyone left, the boys took my husband and me to a place that was special to them where they would go dirt bike riding. We spread his ashes there together, then the boys shared more stories they didn't think were appropriate at the memorial service. There was more laughter and a few tears but it was a wonderful day. I know Josh was present laughing with us. It was such a gift to know how loved he was.

After the memorial services, my grieving process began. I cried until I had no more tears and then I cried some more. I am a person of action and couldn't merely sit with my grief, so I reached out on Facebook® and found support groups. GriefShare® and Compassionate Friends® were recommended and I attended the meetings in person, too. The support I found from others was invaluable in my healing process. My amazing husband was my rock. My surviving children, Tim and Kristina, shared their grief with me. We Skyped®, cried together and shared stories of Josh. My sister and I had a rocky relationship after our mother died and Josh's death brought us together. We are now closer than we have ever been. Support is so important in surviving this process.

Thanksgiving is one of the hardest holidays for me to endure. My last visit with Josh—the last time I saw him alive—was Thanksgiving 2013. My sons had come to visit us in southern Illinois where we were living at the time. After an extraordinary visit, I hugged Josh so hard. My intuition screamed at me not to let him go, to keep him there any way I could. I pushed the feeling aside, thinking I was only worried about his drive back to Texas. Much later, I realized that the universe was letting me know it was our last time together. Since then, I have learned to listen to my intuition.

Church offered me no solace, so I started searching for other tools to help me in my healing process. Using the oracle card deck and reading "Talking to Heaven" by Doreen Virtue and James Van Praagh, I had my first two experiences with this new world that was opening up for me. The first card I drew was, "I had to go that way." I sobbed again, but going my own way was so true. I also had a reading from an amazing medium who confirmed many things I had been feeling, and signs I had been receiving. Never before had I reached out to a medium but was so glad my husband encouraged me to do so. She has since become an amazing friend. I thoroughly believe that the timing was right for Josh to pass on. His work here on earth was done and his death had purpose. This belief helped me to come to the final stage of grief for me—acceptance.

Meditation aided the calming of my mind and started the process of healing my heart. In the beginning, I used guided meditations and healing music which supported an amazing start to my healing process. Journaling helped me release my sadness, anger and even express happy memories in the pages. Journaling was so cathartic for me. I was able to express my feelings with no concern of hurting anyone. I could say anything I was feeling. I even burned some of the pages in the light of the full moon, sending the negative energy to the universe and transmuting it to positive energy.

Reiki, Qi Gong, crystals and essential oils were the next steps in this journey. Reiki and Qi Gong moved my stagnant energy and helped my body release blocks so I could heal. I became a Reiki Master so I could do self-healing and eventually help others. I learned Qi Gong movements from YouTube® videos. When I felt tears coming, Qi Gong movements helped to shift the energy. I used essential oils and crystals, such as Apache Tear and Rose Quartz to uplift my mood.

In April, 2015, I attended a retreat in Angel Valley (Sedona, AZ) on activating my intuitive gifts, learning more about what intuition is, what intuitive gifts are, and how to turn them on. My intuition really started to open up at this retreat and I began to trust my feelings. I cried so much those four days but, by the end, they were tears of happiness not sadness. Angel Valley is a magical place. Being there facilitated more healing for me.

From grief, some amazing things started to happen for me. With my intuition opening, I began experiencing Josh's presence and had visitations from him during my meditation exercises and dreams. When I need a sign, he gives me one, so I know he is with me even though he is no longer in my physical world. I have been able to find my joy again since losing Josh. He was my baby, my youngest child, the one I spent the most time with.

Finding a blessing in loss is a difficult concept for me, but I was able to find that blessing and purpose, and I've been able to heal from the loss because of my acceptance. My path has not been easy, and my acceptance didn't come overnight. I felt anger, depression and I bargained with myself and the universe. I often thought, "I wish we had made different choices" or "I wish Josh had done this instead of that." But, the results were the same. My son was gone and I had to make the choice between staying stuck in the muck or moving forward with my life and following my purpose. I believe that my sons—Tim and Josh—and I had this agreement before we came to this earth. The lessons I have learned, the tools I have gained, and the compassion and empathy I now have for others who have suffered this same loss are the tools I use to embrace my purpose. That purpose is to help others through their losses—whatever they are. My angels and guides work with me to help others heal from their grief, to find the blessings in their losses and to help them find their ways back to joy. From this, I have been able to find joy in my life and you can too.

An Amazing Journey...So Far
By Marion Andrews

Hello world! Yes, I am excited! I am here. You are here. Hooray! Why am I so excited to be sharing this with you?

What if something I write in this joyful book, just one small idea strikes a resonance in you –sparks a little flame and sticks in your mind – until you must take a look at it? Examine it. See its possibilities. And, wow! Eureka! It gets you so excited that you accomplish that marvelous work, that beautiful painting, that kind gesture, the new program that makes life easier and better for millions – or, even more importantly – to just one person?

You see, the numbers are immaterial. What matters is that I affected someone, something, for the better. And, all because I was given the privilege to write a short essay in this book.

What if your purpose here on earth is as simple as that? I have spent a lifetime searching to understand what my purpose is here on earth. What am I supposed to be doing? Am I walking on my path? Am I fulfilling the contract I made when my spirit came here in this body? I asked all sorts of people to help me understand this. I wanted to fulfill *my purpose*!

I believe we don't get out of our bodies until we accomplish some of our contracted purposes. We may have to come back to work on it again, but at the very least, it is essential we have started on that path.

Looking back over my lifetime (and this is something I can do as I am now in the hallowed years of the seventh decade of living), I see glimpses of what I now know is my purpose. I got married at a young age while I was in full lust mode. I still don't know what that was all about, but I do know some things from 20 years of marriage.

I was blessed to bring three wonderful human beings into this world. I loved everything about that process. I loved being pregnant even though I had terrible morning sickness four to five months. What a graphic demonstration that something exciting and very different was happening in my body. The toxemia, the weight gain – all exciting responses to the changes within my womb. How wonderful is that! My puny physical self had a share in creating, nourishing, and protecting another body, a chalice for spirit to indwell, a loving home for spirit housed in this fragile bag of bones. What a privilege I was given.

Then I *loved* being a mom: teaching, cradling, cuddling, and loving those sweet little individuals along their paths. I taught and guided them to the best of my ability and knowledge at that time. I make no apologies or excuses for the mistakes I made. I did what I did within the confines of the knowledge and experiences I had at that time. All three children have grown up to be fiercely independent souls on their own particular paths.

Although my husband and I parted ways, the marriage allowed me to grow and develop my own mind and style. I hope that he learned as much as I did. I was fulfilling my purpose even though I had no idea at that time what it was.

Looking back, I now see that this was a little glimpse of fulfilling my purpose. One incident that stood out from that time was when I attended a silent women's retreat. Now, if you have never experienced a weekend like that, let me set the stage. A busload of 45 women of varying ages, sizes and backgrounds descend on the retreat house. This is a marvelous place; quiet and serene. You sense the presence of spirit immediately upon entering the house. Filled with wonder and excitement, we entered, registered, and attended our first of the guiding talks in the chapel. The first message was, "Ladies, the silence begins now. For the next 48 hours you may only speak when asking a question or at a talk or if there is a genuine emergency. You may choose to speak privately in your rooms when counselling or seeking counsel. The goal here is to turn within, to listen to that voice of spirit that wants to speak to *your* mind and heart."

I invited a friend on this retreat. She was a younger woman whom I felt guided to accompany me. Late the next night, I heard a discreet tap on my door. I answered and welcomed her into my room. We lay on the single bed, head to foot, and I listened to her. She was troubled; her marriage was in jeopardy. The major problem was that her husband didn't "get" her—didn't fulfill her sexually or intellectually. I was guided to ask these questions: "Have you told him what you want in bed? Have you explained what you need? Your husband is not a mind reader. He is trying to please you but working blind, with limited knowledge and experience. You can help by talking, explaining and making your needs and desires known to him." We ended our short, whispered conversation with a prayer of thanksgiving.

Some weeks later, I received a thank you card from her. She credited our discussion as saving her marriage. Things had improved vastly and they both were much happier as a couple. I accepted her thanks but knew that I wasn't the author of that advice. I was merely the mouthpiece used to help her. In that wonderful, spiritual, silent place, I was used as a conduit of great spiritual teaching. What a wonderful gift I was given! That 30-minute whispered confidence impacted her life hugely and who knows how many others along her path. Isn't that exciting? I *love* being the instrument to affect another's life.

Now, I am sure that my purpose is to teach and to heal. In my humanness, my ego says that I need to find that large, important work I am here to accomplish. But it isn't necessary to be grandiose. A purpose can be as small as touching one life. My path and purpose are filled with many small instances when I have been given the opportunity to influence another's life for the better. That's it! I am always looking and asking, "What am I supposed to be doing here?" and "Help me find my purpose," instead of simply getting ego out of the way and allowing spirit to shine forth.

For several years I have walked this road with that dreaded disease, *cancer* – specifically, colon cancer. When it was first discovered, it was already at Stage 3B which meant there was a growth in the ascending colon and active cells had penetrated the colon wall and were growing in some lymph nodes scattered around my abdomen. Say what? I was shocked when I heard this. I was the only one of eight children who ate whole grains and lots of fiber, drank plenty of water, and didn't smoke. What was going on? And yes, I had regular colonoscopies. My latest, only 2.5 years prior, was perfectly clear with no polyps and no signs of disease. After my shock subsided, my thoughts were, oh okay then, what do I need to learn from this? Obviously, I wasn't listening to my spirit; my body needed to do something drastic to get my attention. And it did.

The adventure – the amazing journey – began. Checking in with myself, this didn't seem to be the time of the end of my human form, but rather, a unique opportunity to learn some lessons and then perhaps, to be able to teach others and help them heal.

As an aside, healing isn't physical. Healing is always emotional and spiritual, *then* physical. The manifestation of the disease shows up in the physical, but the healing is always in our spirit.

In rapid succession, I underwent surgery and had several inches of my ascending colon removed. By the 3rd or 4th day of post-operative surgery, my body still had not adjusted. There were no normal bowel sounds or signs. I was now on an NG (*nasogastric)* tube to pump and drain my stomach since nothing was moving through me. I don't remember how the next miracle came to be, but somehow, I communicated with the woman who had given me a few Reiki treatments. She came up to the hospital and gave me a session of Reiki, invoking Archangel Raphael for healing. Within hours, my body started working. Still, I didn't quite accept the healing. My human brain and ego were slow to understand but my spirit knew this was the next phase of my development and growth.

I started my first chemotherapy treatments on Aug 1, 2014. Chemo was an adventure and challenge to my physical body. Each time I went, the toll was higher, but what a great gift it was to me spiritually and emotionally. But, because I have always been the giver, I had a hard time being the receiver. Now I had no choice.

I was showered with love and kindness. Special people stepped up in my life to drive me to the Cancer Clinic. Others brought food. I received literally hundreds of cards and well wishes. What an opportunity to serve others by accepting their love and care. As another important lesson, we need to be receivers to allow others to give and enjoy that growth.

The side-effects of chemo were really miserable, like the nausea, hair loss, and inconvenience. I discussed my hair loss with others and spent a lot of time thinking about it, trying to convince myself it was no big deal. I didn't care too much. It was only hair and would grow back. But, as with most things I tried to prepare for, I couldn't know how I'd feel until I was actually at that point...and it started.

Every time I ran my hand through my hair, it fell out in tufts. I made an appointment with a hairdresser who specialized in wigs, scarves, and hats for people who lost their hair either through disease or through chemo. I didn't know what to do or what to choose. I did know that those feelings about losing my hair were new and scary. I'd always taken my hair for granted. It had been thick and easy to deal with my whole life. But dealing with this loss was harder than I thought it would be. I then went to a dear friend and hairdresser for a trim and a short cut as an interim until it all fell out, trying hard to get my sunny outlook back. It would come, but just for the night, I gave myself permission to grieve a little, pout a little, and shed a tear or two. It was just a short detour but it would be okay! I would be back on track, one foot in front of the other, with a positive smile on my face. Every day in this cancer journey was a challenge. Here is a quote from my Caring Bridge Journal that I kept during the treatments.

> *First off, I am feeling sooooo much better. Started to turn the corner yesterday and am flying today. I almost wrote "this week" there but realized what I have is TODAY. Each of us only has NOW. I am working on living for right now! I have always struggled with my weight and I have lived a lot of my life with the thought and plan that goes something like this...I'll do that when I am thinner, I'll be able to do _____ when I am thin, etc., etc. Or when I'm rich, or when I'm retired. BUT what I have is NOW, the PRESENT only. I am living each minute, hour and day to the fullest! Enjoy.*

My journal entry is especially poignant to me today, four years later. The cancer came back two more times and the journey has been a roller coaster ride of chemo, radiation, scans, and numerous doctor visits. I am grateful for every single day and the way this has played out. My journal entry from 2014 reminds me that even when we are 100% healthy and vibrant, all we have is *now*.

Be present.
Be here.
Show up for yourself.

The God of my understanding can be trusted to send the help, direction, and guidance we need. The angels are messengers waiting to deliver it. All we are required to do is show up and be open to receive it.

The Fear Of Happiness
By Lisa Broesch-Weeks

Happiness can be frightening because it removes us from our zones of safety. Whenever I'm in a place of happiness, my fear bubbles up unexpectedly and paralyzes me. I find it so much easier to avoid pleasure altogether. After all, as I've heard so many well-intentioned people say that we can avoid fear by lowering our expectations and minimizing our dreams to avoid pain or disappointment. The fear makes sense, especially when the message has been ingrained into our psyche since mankind's beginning.

"The intention that man should be happy is not in the plan of creation."

–Sigmund Freud

Entire cultures are built around the belief that happiness is an indulgence—and certainly shouldn't be flaunted—as it might create envy in others. The Japanese, Swiss, and American cultures share this deeply ingrained idea. Could that be why so many of us convince ourselves to step away from the threshold of happiness? Could we be denying ourselves bliss because we're afraid of what might happen when we lose it again—or what others might think of us if we dare to reach for it to improve our current reality?

Aside from the social stigma of declaring that we're happy, there's also (for me at least) the fear that if I allow myself to become too happy and engaged I'll suffer greater pain when my happiness ends, which brings me back to why so many of us negotiate our hopes and dreams down to very small, easily managed, low-risk endeavors that will allow us to carefully go about our days until we ultimately arrive safely at our death.

I'll shed some new light here on the topic of happiness.

I mentioned earlier that I once found happiness to be frightening until I realized there was a difference between happiness and pure pleasure. While living life in alignment with purpose and passion, happiness becomes a set point that isn't dependent on the positive feeling or experience that happens *to you in any given moment.* Happiness is a fixed state, whereas pure pleasure (fun, peace, joy, excitement, etc.) will fluctuate—often moment by moment.

Pleasure can be fleeting. But a state of happiness is constant, *if* you're living the right sort of life.

If we can detach from thinking that a positive feeling or experience will keep us feeling happy, and just enjoy the moment without fear of losing our happiness when that positive experience ends, the fear ceases to exist.

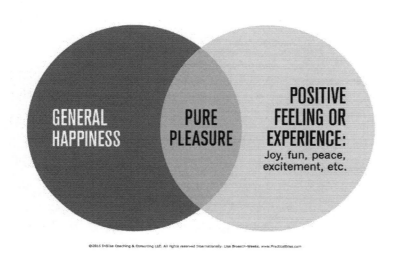

©2016 InBliss Coaching & Consulting LLC. All rights reserved Internationally. Lisa Broesch-Weeks. www.PracticalBliss.com

Look at this "Pure Pleasure" diagram. Notice that when you combine general happiness with a positive feeling or experience, you may induce *pure pleasure.* That moment which is so unbelievably joyous (peaceful, exciting or interesting) isn't to be feared for risk of losing it, because we already accept that it's fleeting. It's to be savored and fully enjoyed!

While on my honeymoon, I had the most amazing time in one of the most beautiful places I'd ever seen. However, the closer I got to returning home, the more anxious I found myself becoming. I was afraid I would never experience that same level of happiness again. By the time I returned home, I was starting to slip into a depression and had to turn to one of my life coaches to sort through my feelings. Why was I feeling so down when I had just experienced my dream wedding and honeymoon? What was *wrong* with me?

I then realized I most likely would never experience that *exact same* feeling of happiness again. But the end of the honeymoon didn't mean happiness had to fade. There would be more pleasures to come and they would all add to the consistent feeling of happiness that I was building. Those pleasurable moments were just the building blocks, not the whole.

Unpleasant things will happen. Yet it's entirely possible to be a happy person – even in the midst of these events. Conversely, amazing things may happen that shift you into a state of happiness, and then subside. That doesn't mean your overall happiness disappears once they're over. In fact, research shows us that by simply *thinking* about past experiences, and feeling gratitude, we boost endorphins and contribute to our enduring happiness.

True happiness isn't dependent upon the universe finding favor and shining down upon us. The universe doesn't care either way—it's not out to get us, and it doesn't have a particular favor toward us. *It's up to us to decide we're going to be happy*, even when we don't get what we want. We can accept and move on, setting ourselves up to embrace the next pleasurable moment.

When you're truly happy, it's like having a diversified portfolio. If one of your investments fails, you don't have to act rashly. You can look at your entire portfolio and see where you can make up the difference with one of your other "investments," keeping your focus on finding new opportunities!

WHAT TRANSFORMATIONS HAVE YOU ALREADY EXPERIENCED

Inspirations: Divine Stories And Intervention, Prayers, Miracles

Perpetuum
By Rhonda Carroll

With wild swings both back and forth
the pendulum moves in rhythm;
a vacillating tilt its course
In confusing perpetual schism.
One side white, the other black
—or is it black and white?
It swings at first both forth and back,
and then from left to right.
We live our lives in alternation
between swings of the pendulum.
We choose our sides of altercation
between everything said and done.
Can we stop the perpetual swing?
We think, but we don't know.
Should we clip its suspension string
to stop its to and fro?
So I wrestle with the yin and yang
of the pendulum's graceful arc
and I gauge the string from which it hangs
to judge what next it marks—
a swing not wide as once before
but with the same momentum.
It won't keep swinging evermore
without my intervention.
But while it swings both back and forth
each apex an opposite reaction
to things with value or with no worth—
a push-pull of attraction,
I must choose 'tween yes and no,
one side left or right,
but can I choose which way to go
if the pendulum halts its flight
and finds a balance in the middle
where certainty stops the run
of swinging through my endless riddle
made by the pendulum?
"I do not know! I cannot see!"

I cry from swing to swing.
I see no more with certainty—
I don't know anything.
There's just one thing I know to do
in the swings of stops and starts;
the only thing I see that's true
is what lies within my heart.
If it's pain from choice I cannot make
I'll give the weight another shove.
I know somewhere between give and take
the answer lies in Love.

Connecting With Archangel Jophiel
By Debbie Labinski

Thank you for believing in angels. They are beautiful messengers from God. I am overjoyed to share with you that you can connect with angel Jophiel, whom I like to call "Joyful Jophiel." Joyful Jophiel vibrates to the color of vibrant yellow and her wings of light shine like sparkles of the stars. Joyful Jophiel is always available to connect with you, when you are in need of creative ideas, beautiful thoughts and joyful emotions.

When you connect to the vibration of Jophiel, you will experience what I call a feeling of euphoric grace. You may feel light, like a flying fairy with amazing wings to take you into your creative journey. It is pure magic! Archangel Jophiel would love to remind you that joy is the highest expression of emotion God has granted upon your soul. Allow Jophiel to surround you in a beautiful cocoon of light and love. When you are ready to go, she will let you fly into your creative self and enjoy the beautiful gift of your nature. You are whole. You are a miracle. You are a wonderful soul of amazing, beautiful, joyful waves that will help so many people who are in need of your love. She wishes you so much joy and thanks you for sharing your moment of bliss with her! Come again as you wish!

Prayer For My Happiness

By Misty Proffitt-Thompson

Dear Lord,

Thank you for the guidance you have been showing me on a daily basis.

I continue to be grateful for the experiences you have provided so I may be able to grow spiritually and understand my true self.

This is my excursion to happiness.

I must remember that those who I consider dear—whether it is my family, extended or close, friends, colleagues or acquaintances—are all here to teach me what is needed for a happiness breakthrough.

At times, their words or actions may hurt me.

It is that experience that is teaching me to grow.

With Your sustained guidance, I will accomplish those lessons I find on my path, and I will become a bit happier on my quest, until another moment of clarity occurs, thanks to Your blessed love.

I so appreciate that you continue to work *to me, through me, and with me;* guiding me to live in the love and light of happiness.

Prayer For Acceptance
By Kimber Bowers

Spirit
Creator of all that is good
Thank you for the blessing of this day.
Allow me to accept the beauty in all of your creation—
the light of the sun, the colors of the field, the aroma of the flowers, the
rhythm of the sea, and yes,
Allow me to accept the beauty of *me*.
I trust the infinite nature of your love.
I trust my own worthiness.
I trust the unfolding of your love through all that *is*.
Letting all definitions fade,
I stand in communion with all in this moment—
Opening my heart to receive that love, welcoming all possibilities.
I allow that love to move through me.
Now and always.
With great peace and great joy.
Amen.

God's Voice Mail
By Bonnie Larson

Our community is small; nine hundred people near the Canadian border, in mountainous northwest Montana. The Kootenai River flows as freely as the helping hands in a neighborhood so tightly knit, you know everyone.

One afternoon, Jerry walked through our door to purchase tongue-and-groove pine paneling. Clearly, he was troubled—very troubled. The previous weekend, he had returned home to Portland, Oregon; discovering his wife, Sue, deeply in stage four chemotherapy. Sue was emaciated and had no hair. Shocked, he knew the seriousness of the situation.

Assisting him in the selection of boards, I "heard" the angels ask me to tell him everything was going to be all right. *Clearly, it isn't, I thought.* Hesitating, I heard them again. The third time, I felt a nudge from behind. Then, a push, as if to say, "Get going."

"Jerry," I said, touching his shoulder lightly, "Everything is going to be all right."

Sue passed away a short time later. Barely able to raise himself from his chair, Jerry suffered grief and deep despair for several months at his Montana cabin in the woods.

One day, he returned to our store. Admiringly, he complimented my beautiful, olive skin—just like Sue's skin.

"No, Jerry. I am sorry. I am not for you," I told him.

Head down, chin resting on his chest, Jerry started talking. For forty five minutes, he shared his love of Sue, his grief and heartache.

I listened.

As he spoke, I heard the name,

"Sharon." I said her name, softly. Shortly after, I heard the name "Sherry." I spoke the name, barely above a whisper. Moving more deeply into the conversation, I heard the word "Texas," then uttered it quietly.

Abruptly, he was silent. Following a long pause, he looked deeply into my eyes.

"I've been trying to determine how you know so much about my personal life," Jerry stated. "This is information only I know. There is no possible way for you to have gathered this information."

He paused. "The only explanation I can think of is that you must be inspired."

With a slight, understanding smile, I nodded.

Finally, Jerry spoke. "Her name is 'Sharon,' but she goes by 'Sherry.' She's not from Texas, but we did meet there."

He took a long drink of water, then added, "We were so in love, but her family said I wasn't good enough. We were young, so we followed our parents' advice and parted. We both married other people and had children. All these years, I loved my wife dearly. Occasionally, I thought of Sherry. I hoped she was happy."

"Jerry, I think it's time you find Sherry," I encouraged.

"I believe it is."

Several months later, Jerry walked through our door. Beaming with a beautiful woman by his side and said, "I'd like you to meet Sherry."

Sherry hugged me tightly, her lovely, dark brown eyes filled with tears.

"All these years I've loved him, and you sent him to find me," she said.

Slipping a beautiful, heart-shaped gold locket with an embossed cross into my hand, she said, "From our hearts to yours. We are engaged to be married! How can we ever thank you?"

"I am so happy for you, Sherry," I replied. "But truly, I was simply God's voice mail!"

J.O.Y.
By Kimber Bowers

J.O.Y.: Just Open Yourself

Joy is a place of wholeness, a place of infinite connection that allows you to embrace your "becoming" without doubt, without fear, without judgement. It allows you to open yourself to the experience and trust whatever may come.

That sounds great, I know, but how do we get there?

We make a choice to own our needs, our perceived missteps, and our experiences. We choose to learn all we can through them. We choose to experience our beauty in growing as we progress. We make a choice every moment by opening ourselves to the experience within and believing that there will be positive growth through it. We make a *choice* to *open* to each moment as the *gift of love* it is, no matter how harrowing it may seem. We make a choice to recognize that we are a part of divine creation, originating from the same awesome source as that fiery sunrise, majestic mountain, or gentle breeze. And as such, we too are awesomely beautiful!

Think about a place where you are most happy, most joyful. It is likely a place where you are without expectation; unattached to the outcome and open to the experience; a place where you feel connected, a place where you are sensually engaged—feeling, hearing, seeing, and fully experiencing all of the inspiration of the moment.

I like nature because I have no expectations of it and I am awestruck by its beauty. Nature awakens all of my senses, grounding me in the experience of the moment. I recognize my part in it, without any expectation of how it "should" behave. I recognize myself as a part of this natural force and beauty.

I like cooking because it is a place where I am open and flexible. I adjust and adapt as I go without expectation of a specific outcome, learning through each step.

I like playing because it accomplishes no goal! I am engaged in play for the pure thrill of it!

All of the things that bring me joy involve this open engagement.

On a deeper level, when I can bring that state of openness to any other event, regardless of whether it is something I would normally regard as "happy," I am able to find joy with whatever is. Even in the middle of a fast-paced chaotic day, when I allow myself to see the beauty of my surroundings, maybe just look up at the sky on the way to the car, I can totally transform my experience. Bringing my awareness to my senses as I do even mundane things like take out the trash or put on the bed sheets, builds my appreciation for the life I am living and allows greater inspiration to come!

Where are you most open? How can you bring that state to other things in your life?

Inventory The Pantry Of Your Heart
By Laura Rudacille

How's your heart?

Your heart was designed on purpose to expand with love and joy; a resilient muscle intended to take a hit then recover and triumph, while maintaining an infinite capacity to preserve memories—forever.

Like a kitchen pantry, your heart is ready for anything, but when was the last time you took inventory of the pantry of your heart?

Are you content and carefree? Are you weary? Overextended? Guarded? Are you rested? Open? Loving? Are you harboring hurt feelings? Lonely? Longing? Are you faithful? Vibrant? Are you sad? Angry? Are you full of joy?

Joy is easy to see. We buy in bulk and stockpile our delight and happiness on the tidy, eyelevel, shelf right in front. What about the dusty and expired items in the back? Old hurts and disappointments? Worry and Insecurity? What are you holding on to that needs to be refreshed or released?

One at a time, examine the issues taking up space and set them aside. Some will be easy to toss out, others will require more consideration.

Embrace stillness; quietly invite yourself to the truth table.

Begin with grace and gratitude. Look to the abundant store of joy and happiness and be thankful. Reach to the back and begin to resolve and remove, creating a path to openness and healing. Invite peace, patience, and understanding and make room for love and wholeness.

Prayerfully meditate over your heart's pantry; close your eyes and lay your hand over your heart.

Heavenly Father, come into the room and enter the pantry of my heart.

Wash me in gratitude for the countless blessings and joy lining my shelves, as I sit in the stillness; in the quiet; and wait to hear your voice.

Allow me to be aware of places of worry, insecurity and concern, as I sit in the stillness; in the quiet; and wait to hear your voice.

Help me to acknowledge the experiences of sadness and hurt taking up room in my heart's pantry, as I sit in the stillness; in the quiet; and wait to hear your voice.

Give me strength to lift them gently, and set them to the side on a shelf by themselves, as I sit in the stillness; in the quiet; and wait to hear your voice.

Fill my heart's pantry with peace, patience and understanding,
as I sit in the stillness; in the quiet; and wait to hear your voice.

I welcome every ingredient You choose. Enrich me, enhance me and encourage me;
as I sit in the stillness; in the quiet; and wait to hear your voice;
as I sit in the stillness; in the quiet; and wait to hear your voice;
as I sit in the stillness; in the quiet; and wait to hear your voice.

Amen

Divine Messages From The Mother
By Kimber Bowers

After a long trek up the mountain, I am sitting in a crevice between sandstone and red rock enjoying the protection of the shade. The sky is blue and wide and clear, but I can barely see it from here. I stare out through a small crack between the mountains and I notice the golden ray of light pouring through it, illuminating the undergrowth in the shadows. Light always finds a way and nature always calls me to be present. No matter what chaos ensues in my life, I find peace here. I am able to trust in the larger plan without needing to understand. I step back from all my need to "do" and "fix" and acknowledge that I do not know what is best. I allow the sand to slide through my fingers and I feel its solidity, resiliency and adaptability. I feel its strength.

Mountains don't start out as mountains. They grow, erupting from the earth's core and scaling the sky. Sometimes they fall. Boulders crash, stone crumbles from pebbles to sand, but even these tiniest granules know their strength. A pebble does not identify itself as a pebble. A pebble knows only the solidity of rock. The majesty of the mountain top is just as apparent as the ease with which this sand flows through my hands. There is no resistance to change here, only allowance. There is no fight to stay the same. There is only growth. There is only becoming. There is only strength.

Years ago, while struggling to support the man I love in his battle with addiction and mental illness, for weeks on end, storms that never rained a drop brewed in the desert. I listened at my window to the frantic cry of desert rock beating against the wind, knowing that even the mountains resist their own crumbling. And I knew they echoed my pain, encouraging me to give a little, to ask for help, to trust in the love that was available if only I would ask. The mountains saw me. The wind understood me. Together they supported me as my every dream came crashing down. The fight did not end the way I had prayed it would, but the mountains reminded me that change is inevitable and encouraged me to find my place in it while acknowledging the pain of surrender. Alone and grieving, I put my trust in the whispers of the wind, the solidity of the stone, and the persistence of the ancient Joshua trees. I accepted the promise of new growth and the greater love unfolding through even the most horrific change. I allowed myself to be stripped of everything I *thought* I was, and I found the strength flowing through my own soul.

The mountains ground me. They remind me that change does not have to be struggle. No matter what state I am in, they call forth the strength of my spirit, pebble to peak, which never fades. The endlessly beautiful sky reminds me of the infinite love that is available with the simple decision to open up to it. What in nature reminds you of your strength? What in nature encourages you to allow that love in?

Nature always speaks to us; through the blowing grass that tells us we can bend without breaking, the flowers that allow the bloom of their own beauty in all conditions, the leaves that let go with such graceful trust that they will be born again, the sun that never stops shining—always rising no matter how dark it may get—the ebb and flow of the ocean reminding us that waves do pass, and the open and trusting adaptability to whatever wind may come.

When you are struggling, go outside and open yourself to whatever *is*. It constantly changes but always expresses glory. Accept the beauty of nature in whatever way it moves without attempting to control it. Accept what comes without expectation. Observe in awe without needing to contain. When we allow nature to move us, we allow the same loving spirit that moves through this beauteous creation, to flow into our own hearts and our own lives.

Let nature speak to you and embrace the message. Feel, see, hear, smell, taste and touch it. Let nature tell you of your greater truth, your greater beauty, and the *one* consistency—the *greater love* flowing through all.

Mirror, Mirror On The Wall
By Kyra Schaefer

There was a time in my life when I was severely depressed. Everywhere I looked I saw nothing but sadness and pain. I heard people talking about how bad things were. I listened to the news showing me the world falling apart. There was evidence everywhere that continued to reinforce my bad feelings. Any time I looked in the mirror I saw nothing of importance or significance. I was tired of feeling badly, so I decided to go against my programming. Every day I woke up and looked in the mirror and said "I am beautiful." What happened next was surprising.

Day 1: Looking in the Mirror

Kyra: I am beautiful.
Kyra's mind: That's a lie, you're disgusting and ridiculous. This is a stupid exercise.
Kyra: I guess you're right, I'm not beautiful.

Day 2: Looking in the Mirror

Kyra: I am beautiful.
Kyra's mind: You've got to be kidding me; this crap again? I'll never believe that, just look at yourself. Stupid.
Kyra: Uh, I'm not sure about this exercise.

Day 3: Looking in the Mirror

Kyra: I am beautiful.
Kyra's mind: Seriously? Didn't you hear me? You suck.
Kyra: You know what, shut the hell up. I'm tired of you telling me who I am.
Kyra's mind: Well what good is this doing? You still aren't good enough.
Kyra: I don't care what you think. Back off.

Day 4: Looking in the Mirror

Kyra: I am beautiful.
Kyra's mind: Ugh...
Kyra: Zip it!

Day 5: Looking in the Mirror

Kyra: I am beautiful.
Kyra's mind: Fine. You're okay, I guess.
Kyra: Damn right!

Day 6: Looking in the Mirror

Kyra: I am beautiful.
Kyra's mind: Hmm, that feels pretty good.
Kyra: That's right! I am beautiful. Say it, bitch. Beautiful!
Kyra's mind: Okay, okay. You're beautiful.
Kyra: Say it like you mean it.
Kyra's mind: *You are beautiful*! Happy now?
Kyra: Almost.

Day 7: Looking in the Mirror

Kyra: I am beautiful! (dancing and twirling around)
Kyra's mind: …
Kyra: Ahhhh, peace.

I think the process took more than seven days, but it is possible to consciously recondition the subconscious mind by going against that inner programming that consistently puts you down.

Another way to go against your programming can be very simple. You could take a different route to work. You could take a trip somewhere you've never been. If you usually say, "No" to going out with friends, say, "Yes" instead. If you are a people-pleaser like me, start saying "No" to people who take from you.

You benefit from going backwards to going forwards. You benefit from going completely opposite to your normal patterns.

I have a client who always puts everyone else first, even when it hurts her career or her health. She has put the needs of her boss, her husband and her children first. You may think to yourself, "How selfless, how amazing, she must feel good to be such a giver." Well, there's a difference between being full of love and happily giving of yourself and being asked to do too much and saying yes when you need to say no.

172

She has been in the hospital and, admittedly, felt it was a nice break where others finally put her needs first. She felt taken care of. This is the most common thing I've seen in women who consistently sacrifice their happiness for others. They make themselves ill so that they can get away from it all.

Can you imagine always doing something you hate just to make sure everyone else was happy? It's like eating poop because everyone else wants and expects you to do it and like it!

This truth is counterintuitive. Doing more for others and caring less for yourself actually contributes to those people you serve feeling less loved, not more.

My client decided to fight her programming. She made a choice that immediately put her into a state of anxiety. This is normal. *Anyone who goes against what they've always done may feel uncomfortable at first, but that doesn't mean something good isn't happening.* It profoundly changes your brain. It changes your environment and others' responses to you.

At first you will feel shaky with this newfound confidence to care for yourself. Then, people will notice they are making their own breakfasts, washing their own clothes, finishing their own projects, watching their own children and overall, being inconvenienced by you not doing what you've always done— taking care of their every need. You may encounter some resistance; stay strong.

They will learn a very important lesson—one that everyone has to learn. You rob them of self-reliance by sacrificing yourself.

When I was three years old, my father was killed. He made choices that consistently put him in physical danger. That's all that needs to be said, because it isn't as important to me as my mother's reaction to his death and what it meant to my self-reliance.

My mother admitted to me recently the reason she was strict and made me do so much as a child was because she was afraid that if something happened to her, I would have no one and would be left alone to fend for myself. This was a tremendous gift she gave me. I can't imagine I would lead the blessed life I do without the lessons she taught me.

I knew how to cook, do dishes, fold clothes, dust, start a fire (with gasoline, but that's a different story), vacuum, manage money (if something looks the same and costs less, go for the less expensive), change diapers, and feed babies (how much and how often). I knew how to paint walls, and deep clean carpets. I learned how to make money in a variety of ways that cost nothing but time and elbow-grease. I knew about death, and how pets come in and out of our lives like people do; so love them as much as possible while they are here.

I learned that people aren't always trustworthy, but as long as you know how to defend yourself, people won't take advantage of you. It may sound bad, but it helped me to be in alignment with myself and remember that as much as I love people, there are still folks that are confused about their self-worth and will rob, cheat and steal to get what they want.

I learned all of this and consistently practiced it by the time I was eight years old. I was an expert, as long as I didn't have to reach things too far above my head. Even then I would climb on the counter top and get whatever I wanted.

It wasn't always fun, because it took work. I only did it because I wanted to please my mom. Believe me, I gave my mom the normal grunts and groans from any child, but she didn't care. She created some significant consequences if my simple *desire* for her love wasn't enough.

No matter how others grunt and groan at you for encouraging them to be responsible, requiring them to treat you with respect, and simply loving yourself more in the process, your friends and family will feel more loved as a result. There is no love in a "sacrifice-win" situation. Only a "win-win" will feel loving to everyone involved.

Triskelion Provided By Giuliana Melo

This is a representation of the goddess; the spiraled legs symbolize moving forward. The darker and lighter lines of the drawing represent strengths and weaknesses or Yin and Yang.

Joy With The Goddess Aine (Pronounced An-Yah)
By Giuliana Melo

Joy is one of the highest vibrations, and joy is high energy. Bringing more joy into our lives brings healing.

We are all filled with deep wisdom and knowledge. We all have a sacred feminine energy within us. That divine feminine is the goddess.

Some of us never realize this. But she is indeed there, waiting for us to discover her and acknowledge her. She wants to share your joy. One of the keys to awakening the inner goddess is to believe that she lives within you.

Stop judging yourself so harshly. You are love, light and joy. You are worthy of calling yourself a goddess, for you are part of the divine. You are made from the earth, the stars, water and air, and have a fire within you that is ready to be ignited and burn bright so that you experience more *joy*.

What is a goddess?
> —*A female deity, a woman who is admired for her beauty. Some have been worshipped in ancient times in various religions and myths.*

What does the word goddess mean to you?

_____

_____

Aine is the goddess of joy. She calls on you to claim your power to heal and experience true joy. Goddess Aine is a Celtic goddess who is also the mother and queen of the fairies. She helps us bring more joy into our lives. Ask her to help you have more fun each day with all your tasks. At this time, ask yourself, "What brings me joy? What did I love to do as a child?"

To invoke her, say out loud or silently:
> "Dear goddess Aine, I call upon you now. Please help me bring more joy in

my life. Please help me be more playful and passionate about my joy. I long to feel joy. Help me bring it to me and through me so that others can share in my joy. Thank you. And so it is."

Aine says: "Joy is indeed everywhere. Find a way each day to experience it. Create space in your day to do something that brings you joy. Connect with nature, go for a walk and allow all of your senses to open up. You are alive and the earth is your playground. Life is waiting to be experienced with more joy."

Aine reminds us that joy is only possible when gratitude and appreciation exist. What do you appreciate right now? What are you grateful for? Appreciation grows—it is the law of appreciation. It is said that not every day is good, however, we can find good in every day.

List 3 things you are grateful for:

_____

_____

_____

Ask yourself these questions:

1. Do I feel joy in my life?

_____

2. Do I love being in nature?

_____

3. Do I take time each day to play?

_____

4. Do I know I have an inner child within me wanting to be noticed?

_____

Our hearts and our souls long to feel joy. Joy is needed so we can open our hearts to more love. When was the last time you had an adult playdate? When was the last time you laughed like a cuckoo bird? When was the last time you colored? Painted? Sang? Danced?

Is your life out of balance? Are you "all work and no play?" Then, now is the time to gather your friends and do something fun. Participate in an activity that brings you joy. Be spontaneous. Ask for divine guidance. Be open to possibility.

"What does joy mean to me?"
Exercise: Connect with your inner child.

What brings me joy?

_____

What activities do I enjoy?

_____

What would bring me joy?

_____

Do I feel I am deserving of joy?

_____

Remember that joy—being a high vibration—evokes more joy in others when you feel it and live it. Then we are pleasant to be around and we attract people, places and experiences to us for our highest good.

Kindness and being of service brings joy. In the spiritual community we say, "When you get nervous, focus on service." Find a charity that you love and volunteer.

How can I be of service today and in the future?

_____

_____

Free yourself from negative thoughts, beliefs and actions. Every time a negative thought arises, acknowledge it and replace it with something positive. You are responsible for creating your day and life. Bring joy each day into your life. Notice the blue sky, the colors of the flowers, birds singing and people laughing.

Focus on what you want. Since I have allowed more joy into my life, people notice it. My energy is joyful. It doesn't matter what you are experiencing, joy helps you shift from fearing to trusting that all is well.

Ways to bring joy in:
1. Wear happy colors
2. Go somewhere new
3. Spend time with children
4. Learn something new
5. Listen to music
6. Play with your pets
7. Watch a comedy
8. Create something
9. Give hugs
10. Be with friends
11. Seek a relationship with the Creator

Passion = joy

What is my passion?

_____

_____

Another way to bring joy in is to create a "happiness" vision board.

Creating a "Happiness" Vision Board

Our dreams and desires are sacred and holy because they come from *spirit*. As with every intention you create, you must learn to step aside and allow the universe to bring happiness to you! Your job is to *ask, allow, believe, and receive*. Your job is not to figure out how. How is up to the universe. Your job is to release, surrender and *trust* that happiness will come. Get happiness out of your head and *feel* how it is to have what you dream, desire, and wish for.

A great way to bring dreams into reality is by creating a "dream vision board" or a "dream vision journal." This will help you *focus* on what dreams you wish to transform into reality. It will help you be more clear and specific about what you wish, dream and desire, and what you wish to be, see and do! Here is what to do:

- Grab a board or journal.
- Intend to bring in more joy, and begin to create the board or journal.
- Using stickers, markers, glitter, photos, cut-outs, words, etc., decorate your board or journal.
- You may wish to display it in an area you occupy each day.
- Feel how joyful and happy you are when you manifest your dream into reality.

Another step to joy is loving yourself. Do you love yourself unconditionally? What steps can you take right now to bring more love in?

_____

_____

_____

As you learn to listen to your heart and as you love yourself to promote healing, you will radiate more joy. Ignite that inner goddess. You are perfect as you are.

Some joy affirmations are:
- I deserve joy.
- I am an original and there is no one else like me.
- I am creative.
- I create with joy.
- I am worthy of joy.
- I deserve to be happy.
- I celebrate my inner child.
- I have an endless amount of creativity within me.
- I am beautiful.
- I am loved.

"When you do things from your soul, you feel a river moving in you. A joy."
—Rumi

Smile! Smiles are free and are understood in every language. Go out today and offer your smile as often as you can.

Draw Your Dream
What Do You Want To Create In Your Life?

Vicky Mitchell Memorial

In the short time that I knew Vicky Mitchell, I experienced the joy, light and compassion that she *is*. Through her unyielding and unquestioning support, I am now showing up in the world a little brighter, a little lighter and with a deeper trust. Thank you, Vicky, for the ripple of light you so authentically facilitated; I am committed to continuing that flow and honoring your ripple in all that I do.

Love,
Kimber

In memory of Vicky Mitchell who's dynamic energy and aura pull my energy to her in 2015 at healing retreat. We clicked immediately because she was so kind, strong and always generous with her love and advice. She will always be in my heart forever. I will see you on the other side Vicky in the meantime keep my seat warm over there with the Angels! Miss you so much!

Love,
Debbie

Vicky brought so much to my life. She was a gift from God. I met her in personal mentoring and she and I became accountability partners. She and I healed through worthiness issues, wanting to be liked, and giving our power away. We created things together and we learned and grew together. Vicky called herself a "joy bunny" and she really was. I miss her very much.
Love,
Giuliana

Vicky, we write this book in your memory, as you left such a mark on people's hearts.
I first meet you through The Invisible Thread book, and realized how much you enjoyed a good laugh.
Cooking was one of your great loves, and through this we learned to love you.
Kindness was your trademark, and Vicky,
You will be remembered by us as the one with the playful heart.

Love,
Tonia Browne

Vicky, you inspired me to own my worthiness, to love freely, to be aware of my physical body and what I put into it. You helped me see more about myself and what I was capable of in every interaction. It's difficult to write this and realize I wont be able to hear your voice again. To hear you when you shout with excitement about this group of authors coming together to create a book based on your favorite topic, which is Happiness. I miss you all the time, and I know you are still advocating on our behalf to ensure more joy on this earth.

I love you,
Kyra

Dearest Vicky,
I'll never forget your smile and laugh. Most of all, I'll never forget the way you danced through life spreading joy all around you.

I love you, dear.
Alejandria Kate

Author Bios

Alejandria Kate

Alejandria Kate is a spiritual seeker. At the age of seven, she began journaling her life. Writing became a vessel for healing. She believes vulnerability is strength and an open heart is the key to inner joy. Alejandria lives a life of love and kindness and strives to become a better person each day. She's passionate about personal development and uplifting others. She lives near Branson, Missouri with her family and beloved animals. Her blog can be found at www.alejandriakate.com.

Anne Marie Scala

Anne Marie Scala is a writer, speaker and educational consultant who is passionate about teaching people to value the relationship they have with themselves. Her business, "Creating Mindfulness Space Consulting," specializes in mindfulness programs for schools, businesses and communities. Anne Marie is based in northern New Jersey where she lives with her husband and daughters Katie (an aspiring animator whose artwork is featured in this book) and Jennie (who makes it her job to keep the world joyful). To find out more, please visit http://annemariescala.com.

Bonnie Larson

Bonnie Larson is a lay minister, reiki healer, healing minister, poet, historian, published author, philanthropist and accomplished business executive. Her passion is to share insights and bridge the gap among science, religion and spirituality—enabling you to realize your highest possible potential.

Christine Salter

Christine Salter is a Psychic and Evidentiary Medium, Spiritual Teacher, and Healer who is passionate about assisting grieving people in opening their own spiritual gifts of spirit communication. Her kind and compassionate approach encourages people to explore their connection with spirit, including loved ones who have passed, while gaining trust in themselves that they can. Christine is dedicated to supporting people on their spiritual and healing journey so that they may re-claim their inner light that was dimmed by the passing of a loved one.

Debbie Labinski

Debbie Labinski is an Amazon best-selling author. She creates a clear channel though her angel intuitive gifts and mediumship readings to guide you on your life purpose. Debbie is passionate about sharing and teaching, and about the empowering messages and the higher frequencies of the archangels, your spirit guides and your loved ones. Debbie is truly inspired that her work will always revolve around helping others to remember their truth with an open and joyful heart. You can find Debbie at www.DebbieLabinski.com and on Facebook @DebbieLabinskiJoyfulAngel.

Giuliana Melo

Giuliana Melo is a spiritual teacher, author and speaker. After going through a diagnosis of cancer in 2011, Giuliana embarked on a healing journey and has discovered that love, light and joy are necessary to live a full life. Giuliana lives in Calgary, AB with her husband and has a 20-year-old son. Giuliana deeply thanks Lori Farrell of Twisted Art Designs in Phoenix, AZ for designing the Joy Color Sheet, and Wendy Hamilton of Wendy Hamilton Art for the creation of the goddess emoji. You can find her at www.giulianamelo.com.

Kimber Bowers

Kimber is a Mind-Body Wellness speaker and teacher who encourages others to discover and embrace their own power to create and navigate change while facilitating growth through that process. She connects with others in an honest and humble manner that inspires insight into their own experiences. It is her purpose in this life to serve as a reflection of the Love that IS, allowing others to discover it within their own realities and within their own souls. Kimber is a Reiki Master, Soul Coach and Clinical Hypnotherapist who can be found at: www.lovinglighthw.com, https://www.facebook.com/lovinglightholisticwellness

For a daily dose of joyful inspiration, join her FREE group The Joy Coalition @ https://www.facebook.com/groups/thejoycoalition

Kimber's Young Authors

Ciara Bowers, 4 years old, is a passionate dancer, artist and lover of all things fluffy or pink. She hopes that everyone reading this book gets to enjoy "a special birthday cake and a cup of ice cream" this year. Isaac Bowers, 9 years old, is an avid reader and coder, explorer of nature and lover of video games. He aims to be an evolutionary scientist one day. He hopes to bring happiness to others through his contributions to this book, as well as through the connections he forms in his day-to-day life.

Kyra Schaefer

Best Selling Author, Motivational Speaker, Writer, Publisher and Rational Optimist. Kyra enjoys exploring the areas of psychology and helps others believe in themselves, to move past limitations and create a more magnificent future. She is the owner of As You Wish Publishing, LLC and is currently working on another book called "Dangerously Close To Happiness". Visit her at www.asyouwishpublishing.com and on Facebook at www.facebook.com/kyraschaefercreative

Laura Rudacille

Laura Rudacille is an author, enrichment speaker and certified restorative and chair yoga practitioner. She encourages growth-through-sharing and champions women through every season of life. Thirty years in the salon industry taught Laura the value of good listening and human connection. Through writing, enrichment events, and live videos, Laura offers thought, partnering insight and candid humor, shedding light on our similarities, infusing positivity and possibility into every moment. Join her live, Sunday and Wednesday evenings in her private group for women's enrichment on Facebook: the AGR Hen House.

Lisa Broesch-Weeks

Best-selling author, speaker and coach, Lisa Broesch-Weeks works with individuals and organizations across the nation to show them how to stop working so hard for everyone else, while helping them become more productive, energized and satisfied with their personal and professional lives. As a former corporate executive, entertainer and author of the best-selling book, *Practical Bliss: The Busy Person's Guide to Happiness*, Lisa offers exclusive personal coaching opportunities and hosts "The Happiness Retreat" each year where participants bask in pure play, planning and practical bliss! To contact Lisa, visit www.PracticalBliss.com/contact

Marchelle Bentley

Marchelle is a brilliant real-life story teller. She lives in Virginia with her husband and loves animals, the beach and her daughter, Ashley "Kyra" Schaefer.

Marion Andrews

After a lifetime of searching and exploring followed by illness, Marion discovered her true calling as a reiki master, teacher and life coach. Sharing her light and love through online classes and at the Chrysalis Wellness Center, she helps others emerge from their own cocoon and fly as beautiful butterflies. Discover more at http://www.chrysaliswellnesscenter.com or email her at marion@marionandrews.com.

Misty Thompson

Misty Proffitt-Thompson is an author, angel-card reader, mind/body/spirit practitioner, teacher and speaker. She helps those who are struggling to find their purpose feel validated and obtain clarity. She sees her clients individually and in group settings. Visit Misty at www.mistymthompson.com.

Rhonda Carroll

Ronnie is a professional artist, published author and worldwide published poet, winner of the "Editor's Choice Award" and nominated as "Poet of the Year." Her life-after-death journey to the other side changed her life from one of daily struggle to daily acceptance and spiritual growth. Her travels and experiences include studying with the Blackfoot Indians (in their teepees) in Browning, MT, hang gliding in the NC mountains, participating as a stock handler in the AZ rodeo circuit, and traveling throughout the world. Her core belief is that *all* people have the spark of divinity within them—we only need to encourage it to shine. She currently resides in Albuquerque, NM.

Tammy Gamester

Tammy lost her youngest son, Josh, in a car accident. Strong spiritual beliefs helped her to overcome this tragic event that put her on the path to fulfilling her life purpose. She chooses to use the lessons learned from this experience to help others on their journey through loss, showing a new way to live without their loved one in the physical world. As a spiritual grief coach, Tammy uses her intuition and coaching skills to assist others to work through their grief. She incorporates reiki, crystals, aromatherapy and connection to spirit in her healing sessions. Tammy is a 2018 graduate from Southwest Institute of Healing Arts (SWIHA) and has her AA degree from Mesa Community College (MCC). www.bluebutterflyinspirations.com

Todd Schaefer

Todd and his wife Kyra have helped over 4,000 people in the personal development field while creating a multiple 6-figure business in 3 years. Todd mostly spends his time speaking, writing, publishing, business consulting and life coaching. He is most passionate about applying spiritual principles, psychology and his business experience to help business owners achieve the foundations and build the systems for real-world success. Todd is the author of *The Acceptance Guidebook: Spiritual Solutions for Active Minds*. He can be contacted for speaking, consulting and coaching via phone or email at his website: http://www.acceptanceguidebook.com/.

Tonia Browne

Tonia Browne is a bestselling author, teacher and coach. She is a strong advocate of inviting fun into our lives and encouraging people to see their world from a new perspective. Tonia's writing includes coaching strategies interspersed with spiritual insights and personal anecdotes. She takes a holistic approach to change. Tonia has contributed to a number of compilation books. Her first solo book, *Spiritual Seas: Diving into Life*, reached a #1 rank on Amazon.com in both the USA and the UK. Her latest project is, *Mermaids: Diving into Life - An Introvert's Guide to Riding the Waves*. Connect with Tonia at toniabrowne.com.

Made in the USA
Middletown, DE
16 December 2018